PRESCHOOL GAMES AND ACTIVITIES

PRESCHOOL GAMES AND ACTIVITIES

SANDRA ZEITLIN TAETZSCH
LYN TAETZSCH

Fearon Teacher Aids
a division of
PITMAN LEARNING, INC.
Belmont, California

Designer: Winn Kalmon
Illustrator: Barbara Hack

ISBN-0-8224-5605-2.

Printed in the United States of America.

To Bob and Herb,
Eric, Roy, and Blixy,
and to our Parents
—with all our love.

Contents

INTRODUCTION   xi

HOW TO USE THIS BOOK   xiii

I   THE CHILD IN HIS WORLD   1

   1   Family Scrapbook, 1
   2   Who Am I? 3
   3   How Tall Am I? 4
   4   How Much Do I Weigh? 4
   5   Walking Games, 5
        5A   Touching, 5
        5B   Naming, 5
        5C   Colors, 6
        5D   Sizes, 6
        5E   Counting, 6
   6   Sorting Book, 7
   7   How Do Game, 8
   8   Opposite Game, 8
   9   Same and Different Game, 9
  10   Magnifying Glass Activities, 9
  11   Weighing Activities, 10
  12   Tasting Game, 11
  13   Touching Game, 11
  14   What Happens If, 12
  15   Conservation Activities, 13
  16   Candle Experiment, 13
  17   Lima Bean Project, 14
  18   Shadow Games, 14
  19   Absorption-Evaporation Experiments, 15
  20   Paper-Cup Telephone, 16
  21   Making a Thermometer, 16
  22   Leaf Designs, 17
  23   Nature Scrapbook, 18
  24   Month Calendar, 18

II TABLE GAMES AND ACTIVITIES   21

    25   Sorting Objects by Size, 21
    26   Classifying Objects by Size, 22
    27   Identifying Objects by Size, 22
    28   Beads, Spools, and Macaroni, 22
    29   Nesting Pots and Bowls, 23
    30   Same and Different, 23
    31   Spin-the-Bottle Color Game, 24
    32   Spin-the-Bottle Shape Game, 24
    33   Touch and Tell Game, 25
    34   Shape, Color, and Size Games, 26
         34A   Matching Colors, 26
         34B   Sorting Colors, 26
         34C   Identifying Colors, 27
         34D   Matching Shapes, 27
         34E   Sorting Shapes, 27
         34F   Identifying Shapes, 27
         34G   Shapes and Colors, 28
         34H   Matching Sizes, 28
         34I   Sorting Sizes, 28
         34J   Identifying Sizes, 28
         34K   Shapes, Colors, and Sizes, 28
    35   Picking, Pasting, and Coloring, 29
    36   Match-the-Color Card Game, 29
    37   Match-the-Suit Card Game, 30

III PHYSICAL GAMES   31

    38   Parts of the Body Game, 31
    39   Jack in the Box, 31
    40   Box Game, 32
    41   Exercise Activities, 32
    42   Balance Board and Balance Line, 33
    43   Ladder Game, 33
    44   Follow-My-Directions Game, 34
    45   Music Activities, 34
    46   Musical Colors Game, 35
    47   Marbles Game, 35
    48   Ball in the Basket, 36
    49   Circle Games with Colors and Direction, 36
         49A   Color Match, 37
         49B   Color Identification, 38
         49C   Direction, 38
    50   Role-Playing, 38

IV NUMBER AND LETTER ACTIVITIES   41

Number Activities   42

51 Number Tree, 42
52 Number Mobile, 43
53 Number Collage, 43
54 Number Songs, 44
55 Giant Step, 44
56 Let's Count, 45
57 Circle Games with Numbers, 45
    57A Number Match, 46
    57B Number Identification, 46
58 Spin-the-Bottle Number Game, 46
59 Match-the-Number Card Game, 47
60 Identify-the-Card Game, 48
61 Match the Number, 48
62 Number-Shape Activity, 49
63 Piling Chips, 50
64 Card Games, 51
    64A War, 51
    64B Rummy, 51
65 Measuring Activities, 51
66 Money Activities, 52
67 Trace the Number, Print the Number, 53

Letter Activities   53

68 Letter Tree, 53
69 Letter Mobile, 54
70 Letter Collage, 55
71 Labeling, 55
72 Stop-the-Music Letter Game, 56
73 Circle Games with Letters, 56
    73A Letter Match, 57
    73B Letter Identification, 57
74 Spin-the-Bottle Letter Game, 57
75 Signs and Labels Game, 58
76 Match-the-Letters Game, 58
77 Count-the-Letters Game, 59
78 Rhyming Game, 59
79 My Own Name, 60
80 Letter-Sound Book, 60

V CRAFT ACTIVITIES   63

81 Painting, 64
82 Fingerpainting, 66

83   Fingerpaint Snow, 66
84   Spatter Painting, 67
85   Sponge Painting, 67
86   String Painting, 68
87   Folding Paper, 68
88   Collage, 69
89   Playdough, 70
90   Making Prints, 71
91   Building, 71
92   Eggshell Pictures, 72
93   Paper Weaving, 72
94   Papier-Mâché, 73
95   Sand Pictures, 73
96   Paper-Bag Masks, 74
97   Box Sculpture, 75
98   Stabile, 75
99   Shape Jewelry, 75
100   Shape Mobile, 76
101   Shape Figures, 77
102   Building a City, 77
103   Hand Puppets, 78
104   Odds and Ends, 78
     104A   Egg Carton Caterpillar, 78
     104B   Spool Shade Pulls, 79
     104C   Buttons, 79
     104D   Toothpicks, 79
     104E   Popsicle Sticks, 80

APPENDIX   81

Materials, Equipment, and Teaching Aids, 81
Child Observation Chart, 85

REFERENCES   87

Introduction

Children between birth and six years of age are going through a very important period of their lives. This is the time of most rapid learning, when attitudes are developed and patterns formed. Their basic feelings toward themselves, other people, playing, learning, and life in general are established during these years. You, as preschool teacher, teacher aide, or parent, can provide the kind of positive experiences and support so necessary during these first years.

Young children are naturally curious and eager to learn. They want to touch, taste, smell, see, and hear the things around them. All of their play is a learning experience which teaches them about their world and the people and objects in it. Your role is to encourage them to discover and test this world with the security of your presence and participation.

This book provides a variety of basic activities and games designed to help children develop skills and concepts that will ease the transition from preschool to elementary school. Some of the skill areas children should have been exposed to and have a basic knowledge of before entering elementary school are:

- Basic vocabulary: action words (build, sit, run, follow); colors and shapes (red, blue, circle); names of objects (stove, book, toy).

- Speaking in sentences and asking questions.

- Speaking clearly so that others can understand them.

- Listening carefully (knowing what is being said to them; knowing the difference between loud and soft).

- Developing large-muscle coordination.

- Developing eye-hand coordination and finger dexterity.

- Following simple directions.

- Understanding the concepts of same and different; classifying, sorting, and matching.

- Increasing attention span, memory, and concentration.

- Putting things into sequence.

- Counting to 10 and having some understanding of the numbers 1 through 5.

Depending upon the children's interests and abilities, development of the following skill areas may also be encouraged:

- Developing rhythmic skills and a feeling for music.
- Using words related to sight, smell, taste, hearing, and touch.
- Problem-solving.
- Understanding the use of numbers and money.
- Understanding the concept of time (today, tomorrow, later, soon, and so on).
- Being able to complete a task or activity.
- Understanding simple rules and following them.
- Using simple tools (scissors, crayons).
- Understanding some basic phenomena in the world around them: why and how things happen.
- Understanding the relationship of others to themselves.
- Being able to identify with others (sympathy, caring for pets, sharing, and so on).
- Being able to say the letters of the alphabet, recognize the letters on sight, and print some of the letters, particularly those of their own name.

More valuable than the development of any particular skill, however, is self-confidence. Providing children with a simple task at which they can easily succeed is very important, especially during their early years or first experiences with you. As they gradually learn to do more difficult tasks and understand more complicated concepts, their self-confidence will grow with their abilities.

This book can guide and suggest, but nothing is more important than your approach in teaching. You can put children at ease with a positive, relaxed, supportive manner. You can make these activity times periods of fun and sharing, times when you and the children learn and play together. In other words, you make it work.

How to Use This Book

You will find the activities in this book divided into several categories. The Child in His World section develops children's understanding of themselves and their environment, and includes simple science projects. The next four sections contain a variety of games: Table Games and Activities; Physical Games, which require more room; Number Activities to introduce children to basic arithmetic skills; and Letter Activities for letter skills. The Craft Activities section includes creative activities such as cutting and pasting, painting, paper weaving, and building.

Some activities can be begun spontaneously, but others will require planning and preparation. Read and understand each activity thoroughly before presenting it to the children. For instance, if you are going to play a game, make sure that you understand the rules so that you don't confuse the children once the game begins.

Assemble materials ahead of time. They are listed at the beginning of each activity. For the most part, suggested materials will be found around the average classroom and home. Feel free to add or change materials as you see fit. One word of caution: use only materials that are safe to use with young children. Read the labels on all materials that you purchase to make sure they will not be harmful to children.

Prepare the physical space for the activity in advance. A good place to work is very important. For the physical activities, a large enough area, indoors or out, should be available. For craft activities, a washable tabletop is recommended. Covering furniture and floors with newspaper or plastic will protect them from spillage. It is important that the children feel free to express themselves without excessive worrying about spilling and splattering. Set the limits you wish the children to follow before the activity starts so that you will avoid problems and misunderstandings later.

Some attempt has been made to arrange activities from simple to more difficult, particularly with the letter and number games. Especially difficult tasks in all areas have been marked with an asterisk (*) to indicate that they should be tried only after the children have had enough experiences with simpler tasks of a similar nature. Take your cue from the children. If they lose interest quickly, the activity may be too simple or may have been repeated too often. If they do not understand, or cannot do the activity successfully with a little effort, it may be too difficult. It is better to start out with simpler activities and very slowly move into more difficult areas so that the children do not become frustrated with failure.

Variation is also important to maintain the children's interest. As you plan several activities for a particular day, choose some from each area. For example, mix table games with physical activities and crafts. Young children have a short attention span. Don't expect them to sit still for long periods of time. Stop an activity before they are tired or bored. It is best to do this by giving the children a warning first, preferably a few minutes before it is time to put things away. Use a positive approach by mentioning what you will do next. For example, "After we have put away the paper and paints, we will play with puppets." It is important to end the activity properly by leaving enough time for cleaning up. Let the children assist you as much as possible, giving them more and more responsibility as they are able to handle it.

Some activities the children can do by themselves once they have learned how to do them. It's a good idea for them to have a place to keep the materials they will need for these activities so that they can get them out and put them away by themselves.

At the beginning of each activity are suggested vocabulary words for you to use, such as BIG and SMALL. While many words may be listed, begin with only one or two simple words and gradually add new ones, particularly when using words of comparison. For instance, in teaching the words SHORT, SHORTER, and SHORTEST, make sure the children understand SHORT before you start to use SHORTER and SHORTEST. Be consistent in your use of words. If you start out using BIG, don't switch to LARGE. Wait until the children have learned BIG and can use it themselves before you introduce the word LARGE.

At the beginning of the activities you will find a list of some of the skills and concepts that they help develop. By no means are all the skills listed for each activity. By observing the children you will discover the way in which they learn and work and will be able to encourage their growth in new areas. You may find it interesting and helpful to make notes on the children's progress. Use the Child Observation Chart in the Appendix for keeping these records.

Listen to the children and allow them to do the talking as much as possible. Encourage them to ask questions, for this is how they will learn. Rather than expecting them to do every activity exactly as it is presented, leave some room for variation. They may have ideas or interests which may be more rewarding for them at that moment than the original activity. Encourage them to make up words, sounds, pictures, and songs.

Treat the children as you would want to be treated. Speak to them intelligently, clearly, and often. Don't ever talk down to them, as they learn their speech patterns from those around them. Wisely limit your question-asking; but when you do ask a question of the children, make sure that it is one they can reasonably answer. Too many questions will cause them to stop listening to you.

Recognize that the children have worked hard at an activity, and that what they have made belongs to them. Don't expect their work to look as though an adult has done it. Praise their work and display it.

Give yourself and the children enough time to relax and enjoy each activity. If you pick a time when the children are alert, relaxed, and well rested, and allow enough time to proceed at a pleasurable pace, the time spent will be fulfilling and rewarding for all.

PRESCHOOL GAMES AND ACTIVITIES

I
The Child in His World

Who am I? Where am I? Who are you? What is this? How does this
happen? These and many other questions arise daily in a child's mind.
This is how he learns. A child is curious about very basic things that we
take for granted. The color of a leaf, a cloud moving in the sky, or an
ant colony all have importance in his world. He must explore, question,
and discover his environment and the people in it. Help him to find out
for himself. Be available and interested in guiding his exploration into
his world. You may learn something more about yourself and your own
environment in the process.

One of the best ways to enrich the child's background of experiences and prepare him for elementary school is by reading to him, and by
allowing him to handle, look through, and "read" the many books now
available to children. Your local library is a rich resource.

① FAMILY SCRAPBOOK

Materials: Ready-made scrapbook OR looseleaf notebook OR your own
book made with construction or drawing paper, hole punch, and yarn or
string; photos of the child and of his family, friends, and pets; drawings;
crayons; paste; tape.

Preparation: Buy or make scrapbook ahead of time. If you choose a
looseleaf notebook, make sure you have plenty of paper for it. To make
your own scrapbook, punch three holes along one edge of ten or twenty
pieces of heavy paper. Tie with three short pieces of yarn or string.

Skills:* Self-pride and understanding; sense of time and growth; understanding family relationships; understanding descriptive terms such as
WEIGHT, HEIGHT, OLDER, YOUNGER.

*Basic concepts are included under "Skills" in this and later ac-
tivities.

This is an ongoing activity that can be enjoyed throughout the school year. Whenever the child makes a special drawing, meets a new friend, has an exciting adventure, or celebrates a birthday, the event can be recorded in the scrapbook. The following are some suggested activities:

1. The child draws a picture of himself on the front cover. Print his name under it.

2. Print GROWING UP on the top of one page. Under it print the date. Then record the child's age, weight, and height. Each month print the new date, age, weight, and height.

3. Make a PETS page. The child pastes in drawings or photos of his pets. Print their names below the pictures.

4. Make a MY FAMILY page. The child pastes photos or drawings of his brothers, sisters, and parents. Print their names beneath the pictures. This is a good page to date and add to periodically as the family grows older. A FRIENDS page can be prepared in the same manner with pictures or drawings of friends.

5. Print MY FAVORITES on the top of a page. Help the child make a list of favorite foods, games, places, toys, or people. Rather than printing the list, the child might want to paste in a picture he has drawn of each item.

6. Make a BIRTHDAY page. Mark the year of the birthday and let the child paste in drawings or pictures of his birthday activities.

2 WHO AM I?

Materials: Photograph of the child, piece of cardboard or heavy paper, paste or tape, crayon or magic marker.

Skills: Self-identity; practical knowledge of own name, address, age, and telephone number.

A very young child should know his first name, but as a child gets older he can also learn his last name, his address, and his telephone number. The following activities will aid the learning of this practical information:

1. **Who Am I? Poster:** Paste a photograph of the child on a piece of cardboard. Under it in large clear letters print his name, first and last. Bring the poster out periodically and say to the child, "Who is this?" If he answers with his first name only, say, "Yes, it's Bobby Brown. Bobby is your first name and Brown is your last name. Can you say Brown?" As this activity is repeated a number of times, the child will eventually remember his last name and be able to repeat it easily.

2. **Where Do I Live? Poster:** The child draws a picture of his house and pastes it, or a photograph of the house, on cardboard. Under it in large clear letters print the address. Explain to the child that the number you are printing is the same number printed on his mailbox and house door. If possible, show him the name of his street printed on a street sign. Explain to him that this is his address. As with the above activity, bring the poster out periodically and ask, "Do you know whose house this is? What is the number of this house? Do you know what street this house is on?" In the beginning you will have to help him, but after hearing it often he will remember it by himself.

3. **What Is My Telephone Number? Poster:** The child draws a picture of a telephone or cuts one out of a magazine and pastes it on a piece of cardboard. Print the child's phone number below the picture. Point out to the child that these numbers are the same as those printed on the dial of his telephone. An incentive for learning his telephone number might be to let him call home when you may need to relay a message to the parents. Be sure to explain that this is not a toy telephone and is only used to make real calls. A play telephone would be better for teaching a child how to dial.

③ HOW TALL AM I?

Materials: Masking tape, ball-point pen or heavy pencil.

Preparation: Paste a strip of masking tape on a blank wall, reaching from the floor to about 5 ft. in height. Each child will need a separate strip. For additional writing space, you may wish to paste several strips edge to edge.

Skills: Measurement, sense of growth.

1. The child stands against the wall in front of the tape. Place a mark on the tape at the top of his head. The child stands back and sees how tall he is. Mark the date next to the line. Repeat this activity periodically so that the child can see how much he has grown.

2. By using a yardstick or tape measure, you may also wish to mark the child's height in feet and inches. Say, "Today you are 3 feet and 4 inches tall." Show him the 3-foot mark on the ruler and count off the inches with him.

Note: This height information may be added to the "Family Scrapbook" (Activity 1).

④ HOW MUCH DO I WEIGH?

Materials: Bathroom scale.

Preparation: See Activity 3.

Skills: Measurement; sense of growth; understanding WEIGHT, HEAVY, LIGHT.

The child stands on the bathroom scale. Point to the numbers on the scale and say, "See, you weigh 35 pounds. The three and the five mean thirty-five." Print "35 pounds" on the wall tape next to the child's height. This activity can be done periodically following Activity 3, so that the child can see himself growing taller and discover that his weight is changing. Explain that he is getting heavier.

Note: This weight information may be added to the "Family Scrapbook" (Activity 1). This is also a good way to introduce the concept that things have weight. Talk about objects that are HEAVY or LIGHT.

5 WALKING GAMES

Skills: Observing; understanding SAME and DIFFERENT; sizes; colors; textures; naming things; counting.

These games are to be played while taking a walk. The walk may be for a purpose, such as going on a field trip, or simply for pleasure, exercise, and fresh air. The walk may be in city streets, town roads, or country paths. As you walk, encourage the child to collect various objects of nature such as leaves, twigs, stones, or seeds (see Activity 23).

5A TOUCHING

Words to use: Rough, smooth, bumpy, soft, hard, sharp, cold, warm, wet, dry, same, different.

1. At the beginning of the walk ask the child, "How do things feel?" Say, "Let's feel this building," OR "Let's feel the bark of this tree."

2. For the child who does not know the word ROUGH, say to him while he feels the tree, "This tree bark feels ROUGH. Let's see if we can find something else that feels ROUGH."

3. For the child who knows the word ROUGH, say, "Can you find something that feels DIFFERENT than this ROUGH tree?" (Example: a smooth leaf) OR "Can you find something that feels the SAME as this ROUGH tree?"

4. As you continue your walk, find new objects to touch, and name their textures.

Note: For very young children, begin with two simple words such as ROUGH and SMOOTH, SOFT and HARD, or WET and DRY. Use these words throughout the walk. New words can be added in future walks.

5B NAMING

Words to use: House, barn, tree, building, store, bark, leaf, plant, corner, streetlight, rock, and the like.

At the beginning of the walk say, "Let's see how many things we can name. I see a TREE. What do you see?" Let all the children take turns naming things.

(5C) COLORS

<u>Words to use:</u> Red, green, blue, yellow, and so on.

At the beginning of the walk say, "I see a RED barn. Do you see anything RED?" The child must find a red object and name it. Then he gets a turn: "I see a GREEN leaf. Do you see anything GREEN?" Let all the children continue taking turns.

(5D) SIZES

<u>Words to use:</u> Small, smaller, smallest; large, larger, largest; big, bigger, biggest; tiny; little; tall, short; same, different.

At the beginning of the walk say, "That is a BIG building. Can you find a BIGGER building?" OR "That is a SMALL stone. Can you find a SMALLER stone?" Let all the children continue to take turns answering this kind of question.

> Note: For the younger child, you might begin by showing him two similar objects, such as two flowers. Say, "See these two flowers? One flower is BIG (point to the larger flower)." Then find two more similar objects. See if the child can tell you which is the big one and which is the small one. It may take many examples before he will grasp the concept of BIG and SMALL. If the child has difficulty, don't ask him repeatedly, but go on to another activity.

(5E) COUNTING

<u>Words to use:</u> One, two, three, four, and so on.

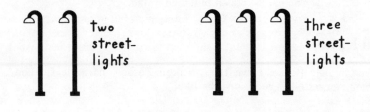

two street-lights

three street-lights

1. Say, "How many red things can you count?" OR "How many trees can you count?" As you walk, the children keep count of how many trees, stores, or other things they see.

2. Another way to play is to say, "Can you find THREE garbage cans?" OR "Can you find FIVE red leaves?" The child must find the right number of objects. With several children playing at once, the object is to find the right number first.

> Note: Be sure that the things to find are at a reasonably close distance and visible to the child.

(6) SORTING BOOK

Materials: Scrapbook (see Activity 1 Preparation), construction paper, scissors, paste, magic markers or crayons, magazine pages for picture-cutting.

1. Big/Small: Print the word BIG on the top of the left-hand page and SMALL on the right-hand page. Cut construction paper into big and small shapes. Let the child paste the big shapes on the BIG page and the small shapes on the SMALL page.

2. Long/Short: Print the word LONG on the top of the left-hand page and SHORT on the right-hand page. Cut paper into long and short strips. Let the child paste the long strips on the LONG page and the short strips on the SHORT page.

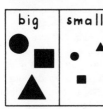 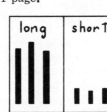 

3. Up/Down: Draw an arrow pointing up in the middle of a page. On the opposite page draw an arrow pointing down. Print the words UP and DOWN on the pages. Let the child cut out pictures from magazines depicting objects that are found in the air and on the ground. Say, "Let's paste this bird UP on top of the page," OR "Let's paste this snake DOWN on the bottom of the page." With the second set of pictures, the child should choose on which page to paste each picture.

4. Left/Right: Print LEFT on the top of a left-hand page and RIGHT on the top of a right-hand page. Look through a magazine for pic-

tures of left-right objects such as feet, shoes, or hands. Let the child cut them out and paste them on the proper pages.

7 HOW DO GAME

Skills: Observing, awareness of the world around, vocabulary.

Ask the child how something goes—for instance, "How does the horn of a car go?" The child responds, "Honk, honk," or something similar. Now the child asks you a question: "How do windshield wipers go?" You answer, "Swish, swish." Let the children continue taking turns asking and answering questions. Some sample questions and answers:

How do wheels go?	around and around
How do birds go?	tweet, tweet
How do cars go?	roar
How do dogs go?	woof, woof

8 OPPOSITE GAME

Materials: Sets of similar objects in two sizes.

Skills: Understanding opposites, observing, making comparisons.

Words to use: Opposite; small, big; sad, happy.

1. First the child must learn what OPPOSITE means. Say, "See this SMALL ball? SMALL is the OPPOSITE of BIG." Now point to another small object and say, "See this SMALL glass? Can you find a glass that is the OPPOSITE of this SMALL one?" If the child points to the big glass, say, "You are right. This is a BIG glass, and BIG is the OPPOSITE of SMALL." He may need much help in understanding this concept.

2. Alter the game to reinforce the idea of OPPOSITE. Say, "I'm going to make a very SAD face and you make a HAPPY face with a big smile. I'm SAD. You're HAPPY. That's OPPOSITE." Then change to a smile and say, "Now if I make a HAPPY face, what are you going to do to be the OPPOSITE of HAPPY?" The child will probably guess that he should make a sad face. Help him if he has trouble. The idea of OPPO-SITE may not be easy for a child to grasp.

Continue expanding into other areas; for example: "If I walk FAST, what will you do to do the OPPOSITE?" Then let the child take turns with you or with other children, making up the first item and letting the other person figure out its opposite. Once the children learn the basic idea, they can play this game by themselves, taking turns making up the first item. They can play the game anytime, interspersed among other activities.

3. Other OPPOSITE words to use are: TALL and SHORT; FAT and THIN; FAR and CLOSE; DARK and LIGHT; HEAVY and LIGHT; YES and NO.

(9) SAME AND DIFFERENT GAME

Materials: Any available objects.

Skills: Understanding SAME and DIFFERENT, observing.

Words to use: Same, different.

1. First the child must learn what SAME and DIFFERENT mean. Point to two glasses (or other objects) that are the same and say, "These glasses are both small, aren't they? They both have a red line around the middle too, don't they? These glasses are both the SAME." Point to two other similar objects and say, "These two plates are both flat and big and white, aren't they? Are they the SAME?" Once the child is able to recognize two things that are the SAME, use this method to teach him what DIFFERENT means.

2. Once he has learned both words, you can take any two objects and ask, "Are these two bowls the SAME or DIFFERENT?" Then ask, "Why?" (As long as the child has a good reason for his definition of SAME or DIFFERENT, accept it. He may think along different lines than the obvious ones we are used to such as size and color.)

3. Another variation is to find objects that are the same and match them.

(10) MAGNIFYING GLASS ACTIVITIES

Materials: Magnifying glass, any available objects.

Skills: Observing, understanding changes in size, eye-hand coordination, identifying and labeling objects.

Words to use: Close, closer; far, farther; large, larger; small, smaller; magnifying glass.

1. Show the child a magnifying glass. Let him hold it. Say, "Let's see what happens when we look through this MAGNIFYING GLASS. Let's look at something CLOSE first." Hold the magnifying glass close to an object, such as a pencil. Say, "Now see what happens as we move the MAGNIFYING GLASS FARTHER away." Move the glass back slowly. The pencil will appear larger.

2. Let the child try looking through the glass himself, moving it back and forth, closer and farther to see how the size changes. Say, "See how the pencil looks LARGER when you hold the MAGNIFYING GLASS FAR from it."

3. If the child asks why the size changes when you look through the glass, give him this simple explanation: The size of the pencil doesn't change. The magnifying glass makes it look different.

(11) WEIGHING ACTIVITIES

Materials: Bathroom scale, balance scale if available, objects of various weights.

Skills: Observing, understanding weight, measuring, classifying.

Words to use: Scale; measure; heavy, heavier; light, lighter; pounds; weigh.

1. If you have a balance scale available, take two objects such as an apple and a grapefruit and ask the child to place one on each side. Say, "See this side go down? That's because this grapefruit is HEAVIER than the apple on the other side." Try different objects of different weights.

2. If you don't have a balance scale, have the child hold his arms outstretched and place a light object in one hand and a heavier object in the other. Say, "Which hand is harder to hold up?" After the child answers, say, "That's because you're holding a HEAVY book in that hand. HEAVY things are harder to hold up than LIGHT things. The paper you're holding in your hand is LIGHT and easy to hold up." Have the child try holding various objects in each hand.

3. If you have a bathroom scale, have the child stand on it. Point to the numbers and say, "This scale says you WEIGH 40 POUNDS. How many POUNDS do you think I WEIGH?" Get up on the scale yourself and let him see the numbers go up. Say, "See, I WEIGH 120 POUNDS. I am HEAVIER than you are." This is a good activity for a small group. Children take turns weighing themselves to see who is heavier or lighter.

12 TASTING GAME

Materials: Foods with a variety of tastes such as lemon, sugar, and salt.

Preparation: Assemble a variety of different-tasting foods on a table.

Skills: Observing, developing a sense of taste, vocabulary of tastes.

Words to use: Salty, sweet, sour, warm, cold, cool, juicy, dry, bitter, crunchy, smooth.

1. Say, "We're going to see how many different ways things can taste. Let's try sugar first." Lick a cube of sugar yourself. Then ask the child to lick a piece. Say, "Mmm, sugar tastes SWEET." Take a piece of lemon and say, "Now let's try this lemon. Just taste a little bit." Both you and the child try it. Say, "Ooooh, this doesn't taste SWEET like the sugar. This lemon is SOUR." Now give the child something else sweet, like a piece of candy. Ask, "Does this taste SWEET like the sugar or SOUR like the lemon?" Now give him another taste of something sour and ask, "Is this SWEET or SOUR?" The game can continue using the other tastes mentioned above.

2. For variation, try smells rather than tastes, or combine the two. Have the child first smell something and then taste it. See how many different smells you can describe.

13 TOUCHING GAME

Materials: Various items with different textures such as salt, flour, rice, beans, water, or ice; several small bowls.

Preparation: Fill little bowls with the suggested items listed under Materials.

Skills: Observing, developing the sense of touch, vocabulary.

Words to use: Touch, soft, silky, smooth, rough, bumpy, cool, warm, icy, sticky, hard.

1. The child places his hand in the first bowl and feels what is inside. Say, "How does the flour in this bowl feel?" The child may answer that it feels "nice." Say, "Doesn't it feel SOFT and SMOOTH?"

2. After two or three different things are felt and described, ask the child to close his eyes. Place one of the three bowls in front of him.

Say, "Let's play a touching guessing game. What does this feel like?"
He may be able to remember, from the feel of it, what is in the bowl and
be able to describe it. If he has trouble, give him some hints or let him
open his eyes.

3. Let the child try the guessing game on you. Close your eyes
and let him place a bowl under your hand for you to guess the contents.

4. Gradually add more items to the game.

5. Let the children play the guessing game with each other.

14 WHAT HAPPENS IF

Materials: Objects appropriate to the selected activities.

Skills: Observing, knowledge of the world and of objects, predicting.

This game is played by saying, "What happens if . . . ." and then
trying the activity described. For instance, "Let's see what happens if
I place this ball at the top of a slanting board." The child guesses the re-
sult, "It will roll down." Let the ball go and watch what happens. The
following are some suggested activities. Encourage the child to develop
his own questions once he gets the idea of the game.

1. What happens if I put salt in water? It melts.
2. What happens if I put a stone in the water? It sinks to the
   bottom, but does not melt.
3. What happens if I drop a cork in water? It floats on top (because it is lighter than the water).
4. What happens if I put a ball at the bottom of a slanted board?
   It stays there.
5. What happens if I hold a feather in my open hand on a windy
   day? It blows away.
6. What happens if I hold a rock in my open hand on a windy day?
   It does not blow away.
7. What happens if I stick my hand in a bowl of water? It gets
   wet.
8. What happens if I stick my hand with a rubber glove on it into
   a bowl of water? The outside of the glove gets wet. The hand
   stays dry.
9. What happens if I stick my hand with a woolen glove on it into
   a bowl of water? The hand and the glove get wet.
10. What happens if I push a swing forward? After I let go, it
    swings backward and forward by itself a few times until it
    gradually stops.

(15) CONSERVATION ACTIVITIES

Materials: Jars of different sizes and shapes, water colored with food coloring, clay or dough, measuring cups.

Skills: Observing, understanding conservation (the amount of water or clay does not change simply because the shape changes), predicting, measuring, pouring.

     1. Fill a one-cup measuring cup with colored water. Say to the child, "We have one cup of water here, right?" Pour the water into a wide jar. Say, "I wonder how much water we have now—less, more, or the same one cup we started with." If the child thinks there is less or more water now, pour the water back into the one-cup measure and show him that it is the same.

     Pour the same water into a narrow jar. Say, "Let's see how much water we have now—more, less, or the same as the one cup we had before?" At first the child will probably think that the amount changes because the water level is higher in a narrow jar and lower in a wide jar. But if you pour it back and forth enough times, eventually he will see that there is the same amount of water in all the jars.

     2. Fill a half-cup measuring cup with a piece of clay or dough. Fill it tight and pack it down flat. Say, "Here we have a half cup of clay." Take the clay out of the cup and form a long snake out of it. Say, "Do we now have the same, more, or less clay than we had before?"

     Continue the clay activities as you did the water activities, letting the child form the clay into different shapes. Then put it back into the half-cup measuring cup, until he sees it is always the same half cup of clay.

(16) CANDLE EXPERIMENT

Materials: Candle, match, jar with a wide top large enough to hold a candle, jar cover.

Preparation: Place a candle in a jar. To secure it firmly, first light the candle. Hold it over the jar letting a few drops of wax drip to the bottom of the jar. Blow the candle out and place it immediately in the wet wax. Hold until the wax is solid.

Skills: Observing, understanding how and why, predicting.

Words to use: Candle, light, fire, air, oxygen, burn, gas.

Light the candle with a match. Say, "See the CANDLE BURN?
Now watch what happens after I put the top on the jar. " Place the top on
the jar. Wait a while. The flame will go out after it uses up all the oxygen in the jar. Take the top off the jar and light the candle again.

Place the top on the jar, but this time remove it just before the
flame goes out. As the flame grows larger again, talk about the fire need-
ing something to make it burn. That something in the air that we cannot
see is oxygen. (You might also point out that we need oxygen to breathe.)

(17) LIMA BEAN PROJECT

Materials: Jar or glass, paper towels, water, several lima beans.

Skills: Observing, understanding how plants grow, direction—UP and
DOWN, patience.

Words to use: Lima bean, seed, water, roots, stem, down, up, top, bottom, grow, germination.

Note: Have the child do as many of the steps by himself
as possible.

1. Line a glass or jar with paper towels. Pour enough water in
to wet the towels completely. Place several dry lima beans about halfway
down between the towel and the glass.
Keep the towels moist. Check the glass every day to see if more
water should be added. After a few days, one or several of the beans
will start to germinate.

2. Talk about the ROOTS growing DOWN, the STEM growing UP,
how the bean is a SEED which uses WATER to GROW, and how we call
this process GERMINATION.

(18) SHADOW GAMES

Materials: An artificial light or natural sunlight, a wall or screen, an
object to use for casting shadows (optional).

Skills: Dexterity, understanding how shadows are made, coordination.

1. As the sun comes in the window on a sunny day, place your
hand between the source of light and a wall or screen. Move your hand
and fingers to various positions in order to form animals, birds, and

other figures. Have the child watch for the shadow on the wall. Then let him try to make the shadows while you watch. The same effect can be achieved with an electric light.

2. You can make a silhouette of a child by experimenting with the distance between the light and the wall. Put a large piece of paper on the wall. Have the child stand sideways in front of it. Point a strong light, a few feet from the wall, toward the paper. Trace the outline of the child's features on the paper.

*(19) ABSORPTION-EVAPORATION EXPERIMENTS

Materials: Shallow bowl or jar-top, sponges, water, milk, oil, paper towels, cotton, blotters, terry-cloth towel, napkin, thin fabric.

Skills: Observing, vocabulary, understanding changes such as absorption and evaporation.

Words to use: Absorb, evaporate, liquid.

1. Fill a shallow bowl or jar-top with water. Ask the child to dip one end of a blotter in the water and hold it there. Say, "Watch how the blotter ABSORBS the water." Try this experiment with other liquids like milk or oil, and with other blotters like paper towels, cotton, or sponges. Show how a fluffy terry-cloth towel absorbs the water faster than a thin piece of material. Explain that this is why we use terry-cloth towels to dry ourselves after a shower or bath.

2. Say, "Water, milk, oil and other things we tried to ABSORB are all LIQUIDS. Besides being ABSORBED by other materials, LIQUIDS can also EVAPORATE. Can you guess what happens after rain collects in a puddle?" The child may figure out that some of the rain is absorbed by the ground. Say, "You are right. Some of it is ABSORBED by the earth and plant roots, but some of it disappears because it EVAPORATES.

Let's see how this happens." Place a little water in a flat dish and put it outside or on a windowsill in the hot sun.

Check the dish from time to time. The water will slowly disappear as it evaporates. Explain that heat makes it evaporate faster. That's why the sun dries up the ground quickly after a rainstorm.

⟨20⟩ PAPER-CUP TELEPHONE

Materials: Two paper cups, length of string, pointed scissors or other tool for making holes in cups.

Skills: Listening, speaking, learning how to use the telephone, vocabulary, learning how sound travels.

Words to use: Telephone phrases: hello, how are you, and the like.

Make a small hole in the bottom of each paper cup. Attach each end of the string through one hole. Knot the string at both ends and pull it taut, keeping it taut as the activity proceeds.

Show one child how he can hold one cup to his ear and listen while another child talks into the other cup.

Note: This activity is a good make-believe game for children to play. They will have automatically picked up words and phrases from adult conversations they have overheard, and will repeat them to each other.

⟨21⟩ MAKING A THERMOMETER

Materials: Piece of cardboard, white and red ribbons, thread for sewing, scissors or utility knife, crayon or magic marker.

Preparation: Sew the white and red ribbons together end to end.

Skills: Observing, understanding how to use a thermometer, understanding changes in temperature.

Words to use: Hot, warm, cool, cold, heat, temperature, thermometer.

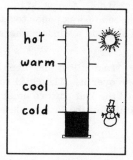

1. Let the children help with this part of the preparation. Explain the details as you proceed: Cut a ribbon-sized slot at the top and bottom of the cardboard. Draw four lines evenly spaced across the cardboard. Print from top to bottom at the side of each line: hot, warm, cool, cold. If you wish, draw or paste on pictures to illustrate the different temperatures. For instance: a sun for HOT, a bathing suit for WARM, a coat for COOL, snow and mittens for COLD.

Insert the white end of the ribbon through the top slot and the red end of the ribbon through the bottom slot. Fasten both ends of the ribbon together at the back of the cardboard with a safety pin. Now the ribbon can be moved freely up and down. The red part of the ribbon shows the temperature.

2. If you have a real thermometer available, show it to the child. Explain how the red part shows what the temperature is, or how hot or cold it is. You can explain that usually mercury is used in a real thermometer.

Say, "It's a very HOT day. Move the ribbon to show us a HOT TEMPERATURE." Help the child at first until he gets the idea that more red should show for hotter temperatures, less for cooler temperatures.

(22) LEAF DESIGNS

Materials: Fall leaves, wax paper, warm iron, crayons, paper.

Preparation: Collect some fall leaves ahead of time.

Skills: Appreciating nature, understanding how heat melts wax, observing leaves (veins and stems).

1. Wax-paper design: The child arranges a few leaves on a piece of wax paper. Place another piece of wax paper over the leaves and press

firmly with a warm (not hot) iron. As you do this, explain how the heat melts the wax on the two pieces of wax paper together, holding the leaves in place. Put the finished sheet in a window where light can shine through it.

2. Crayon rubbing: Take a leaf and place it flat on the table. Place a piece of white paper over it. The child rubs the side of a crayon over the paper and leaf until the leaf pattern emerges. The crayon picks up the veins, stem, and outline of the leaf, making a picture.

 ## 23 NATURE SCRAPBOOK

Materials: Scrapbook (see Activity 1 Preparation); things the children have collected on nature walks, such as leaves, flowers, twigs, and seeds; crayons or magic markers; paste; photographs depicting the seasons; white paper; colored paper; scissors.

Skills: Arranging sets of objects, observing, collecting, sorting, understanding seasons.

Make a scrapbook to keep a record of your nature walks:

1. After pressing leaves and flowers between wax paper, they can be pasted into the scrapbook (see Activity 22).
2. The child draws, colors, or paints pictures in the scrapbook about the different seasons. Or he pastes in photographs depicting the seasons.
3. The child makes a seed picture by pasting different seeds in various patterns on a page.
4. Cut snowflakes out of white paper and help the child paste them on colored paper for a winter page.
5. The child makes a picture by gluing small bits of twigs on a page.

24 MONTH CALENDAR

Materials: Cardboard, white paper, scissors, magic markers or crayons, paste, pictures from magazines or other sources.

Preparation: On a piece of white paper mark off boxes for the number of days in the month. Mark the days of the week (Monday, Tuesday, and so on) across the top and insert the number of each day in the appropriate box. From magazines or other sources cut out small pictures depicting special days of the month, such as holidays or birthdays of famous people.

Skills: Naming days and months, learning numbers, learning about weather and holidays.

Words to use: Monday, Tuesday, and so on; January, February, and so on; Passover, Easter, Memorial Day, and other holidays.

Say, "We are going to make a calendar." At the very top of the cardboard, print, or help the child print, the name of the month. Then let the child color or paint a picture on the top half of the cardboard below the printed name, allowing enough room at the bottom for the calendar sheet. When the child is finished painting, paste the prepared calendar sheet on the bottom of the cardboard. Help the child paste the magazine cutouts in the appropriate boxes, talking to him about the events the pictures represent.

II
Table Games and Activities

Children learn much from games played with others. For instance, games teach impulse control—the ability to share and to wait one's turn. Such control is not easy for a child to learn. It will come with much experience, and patience will be needed on your part to help him.

Allowing a child always to win may later shake his confidence when he plays with others and loses. We all like to win, but learning to lose and be a good sport about it is also important. When playing a game with a child you should allow him to win often, especially when he is very young, but he should gradually learn how to lose once in a while. He should be encouraged to play his best and to play fairly.

The games we have provided are simple. You can expand and change them to meet your needs. Many games are also available at local stores. When buying a game, be sure that it will not be so difficult as to frustrate the child.

(25) SORTING OBJECTS BY SIZE

<u>Materials:</u> Sets of similar objects in different sizes, such as boxes, erasers, jars, paper bags, or stones.

<u>Skills:</u> Observing, understanding differences in size, coordination.

<u>Words to use:</u> Small, smaller, smallest; large, larger, largest; big, bigger, biggest; little.

1. Begin with just two sizes, BIG and LITTLE. Say, "Let's put all these things into two piles, one pile of LITTLE things and one pile of BIG things." Begin the piles yourself by putting one small object in one pile and a large object of the same kind in the other pile. Say, "Can you find a LITTLE box (stone, jar) to put in this pile of LITTLE things?"

2. Once the child has learned BIG and LITTLE, try playing the game with four piles: BIG, BIGGER, SMALL, SMALLER. Eventually you can add SMALLEST and BIGGEST.

26 CLASSIFYING OBJECTS BY SIZE

Materials: Three to ten objects of the same kind, but varying in size.

Skills: Observing, classifying by size, coordination.

Words to use: Small, smaller, smallest; big, bigger, biggest; large, larger, largest; little.

Say, "Let's make a line of blocks (jars, boxes) from SMALLEST to BIGGEST across the table. Which is the SMALLEST block in the pile?" Put this block down at one end of the table. Then ask for the next bigger block to put next to it.

Continue in this manner to form a line from smallest to largest. Talk about the objects' relative size: "Both these blocks are BIG, aren't they? But which one is BIGGER? Which is SMALLER, this block or the one next to it?"

27 IDENTIFYING OBJECTS BY SIZE

Materials: Three to ten objects of the same kind, but varying in size.

Skills: Observing, identifying sizes.

Words to use: Small, smaller, smallest; large, larger, largest; big, bigger, biggest; little.

Pick out an object from the pile and say, "Is this block (jar, box, toy) BIG or SMALL?" Pick up another block and ask, "What about this one? Is it BIGGER or SMALLER than the first one I picked up?"

In this game you are trying to get the child to use the words BIG, SMALL, BIGGER, SMALLER, and so on. Pick up an object and have him try to name its size in relation to other objects which you point out.

28 BEADS, SPOOLS, AND MACARONI

Materials: Beads, spools, or macaroni of various kinds; string.

Skills: Coordination, finger dexterity, forming patterns, observing, understanding SAME and DIFFERENT.

Words to use: Same, different, pattern, design.

1. Stringing: Tie a knot in one end of a piece of string and let the child string the beads, spools, or macaroni. The ends can be tied together to form bracelets and necklaces.

2. Sorting: Place a pile of several different kinds of beads, spools, or macaroni in front of the child. Pick up one and say, "Let's find all the beads (spools, macaroni) the SAME as this one and put them in a pile. Let's put the other kinds in separate piles." Talk about them being the SAME or DIFFERENT.

3. Forming patterns: Take a few beads, spools, or macaroni and place them on the table in a simple pattern. Say, "Can you make a PATTERN (DESIGN) like mine?" Let the child try to copy yours. Then let the child make up a pattern for you to copy.

(29) NESTING POTS AND BOWLS

Materials: Unbreakable pots and/or bowls of various sizes and shapes; water, sand.

Skills: Small- and large-muscle development, understanding size classification, building and stacking skills, coordination, understanding FULL and EMPTY.

Words to use: Build, stack; full, empty; small, smaller, smallest; big, bigger, biggest; little; large, larger, largest.

1. Building and stacking: This is a good activity for the very young child. He will enjoy nesting the pots and bowls inside each other and stacking them on top of one another.

2. Full and empty: Playing with water or sand, the child fills and empties the pots and bowls. Talk about FILLING and EMPTYING.

3. Size: Use pots and bowls of different sizes to play size games such as Activities 25, 26, and 27.

(30) SAME AND DIFFERENT

Materials: Groups of three objects of the same kind, two identical and one slightly different.

Skills: Observing; understanding SAME and DIFFERENT; understanding size, color, and shape.

Words to use: Same, different; alike, not alike; size; color; shape.

Place three objects on the table. Two should look exactly the same. The third one should be different in some way. Say, "Are all these blocks (jars, books) the SAME?"

If the child says, "Yes," ask additional questions about the three objects. For example, "Are they all the SAME COLOR (SIZE, SHAPE)? Is this one as big as these two?"

After the child points out which object is different, ask him what is different about it. Don't expect his answers to match yours. He may respond with a more imaginative answer than your own. Accept his answer as long as he understands what DIFFERENT and SAME mean. Encourage him to observe differences beyond size, color, and shape.

31 SPIN-THE-BOTTLE COLOR GAME

Materials: Narrow-necked bottle; large piece of paper, cardboard, or fabric; crayons or magic markers; construction paper; scissors.

Preparation: Cut a large circle out of cardboard, paper, or fabric such as burlap. Mark it off into eight sections (wedges). Color each section a different color. Cut up construction paper into 2 in. x 1 in. pieces. Cut four pieces for each color on the circle.

Skills: Matching colors, waiting one's turn, following directions.

Note: This game is to be played by two or more children.

Place the circle on the table or floor in the center of all players. Mix up the color cards and divide them equally among the players.

The first player spins the bottle in the center of the circle. When it stops spinning, the neck of the bottle will end up in a colored space. If the player has a card of this color, he places it on the appropriate wedge in the circle. The next player does the same. If a player does not have the color he lands on, the next player has his turn. The object of the game is to use up one's cards as fast as possible.

32 SPIN-THE-BOTTLE SHAPE GAME

Materials: Same as Activity 31.

Preparation: On the circle you made for Activity 31, add a cutout shape to each section (circle, square, rectangle, triangle, crescent, diamond).

If necessary, the shapes can be repeated to fill in all sections. If you use five shapes, cut out twenty-five 2 in. x 1 in. cards and draw each shape on five cards.

Skills: Matching shapes, waiting one's turn, following directions.

Note: This game is to be played by two or more children.

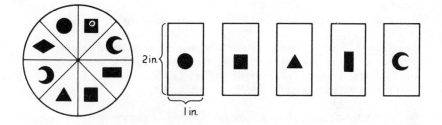

Place the circle on the table or floor in the center of all players. Mix up the shape cards and divide them equally among the players.

The first player spins the bottle in the center of the circle. When it stops spinning, the neck of the bottle will point to a particular shape, such as a square. If the player has this shape card, he places it on the appropriate wedge in the circle. The next player does the same. If a player does not have the shape he lands on, the next player has his turn. The object of the game is to use up one's cards as fast as possible.

33   TOUCH AND TELL GAME

Materials: Any available objects.

Skills: Sense of touch—texture, weight, size, shape; concentrating; naming; speaking.

Words to use: Soft, hard; rough, smooth; heavy, light; big, small; thick, thin.

Note: This game can be played anywhere indoors or out. Play it with one or more children. Once they learn the game, they can play it by themselves.

1. Ask the child to sit down, close his eyes, and open his hands in front of him. Place an object (stone, pencil, leaf) in his open hands.

Ask him questions about the object: "What does it feel like? Is it HARD or SOFT? Is it THICK or THIN? What is it used for? Where is it found? What does it do?" The last question should be, "What is it?" The goal of the game is to figure out what the object is without opening one's eyes.

2. Let the children take turns holding an object and answering questions about it.

 SHAPE, COLOR, AND SIZE GAMES

<u>Materials:</u> Container with a wide top, construction paper, scissors.

<u>Preparation:</u> Cut <u>two</u> copies of the following out of construction paper: four basic shapes (square, rectangle, triangle, circle) in two sizes each and each size in three colors (red, yellow, blue)—a total of 48 cutouts. Save the cutouts for Activity 35.

<u>Skills:</u> Understanding shapes, colors, SAME and DIFFERENT, LARGE and SMALL.

<u>Words to use:</u> Square, circle, rectangle, triangle; large, small; blue, red, yellow; same, different.

 MATCHING COLORS

Mix up the cut shapes in a bowl, box, or other container with a wide top. Take out one shape and ask the child to pick out any other shape of the same color. Say, "Can you find another piece the SAME COLOR as this BLUE one?" Let the child make a pile of the pieces he matches correctly. Continue until all colors are matched.

Note: If the child has difficulty matching colors, play the game first by letting him pick out the shape. You find the color that matches it. Another way to make the game easier for the child is to place only a few of the 48 pieces in the container. It is important that his first attempts be successful.

(34B) SORTING COLORS

Place the shapes in the container. Take out any blue shape and say, "Let's put all the pieces that are BLUE, like this one, in this pile." Continue, making one pile each for blue, red, and yellow shapes.

Note: At this point the child may not yet know the colors
RED, YELLOW, and BLUE, but by using the words
SAME and DIFFERENT, you can help him learn to match
colors.

(34C) IDENTIFYING COLORS

Place the shapes in the container. Say, "Can you find a RED shape
in the bowl?" Continue with all the colors until the container is empty.

Note: Another way to play this game is to pick out a shape
and ask the child to name its color.

(34D) MATCHING SHAPES

Place the shapes in the container. Take out one circle and ask
the child to pick out a piece that matches its shape. Say, "Can you find
another piece the SAME shape as this CIRCLE?" Let the child make a
pile of the shapes he matches correctly. Continue with the matching until all shapes are matched. (Remember, size is not important here. A
small circle can be matched with a big circle.)

Note: If the child has difficulty, play the game by letting him pick out the first piece. You match the shape.

(34E) SORTING SHAPES

Place all the shapes in a pile on the table. Take out any square
shape and say, "Let's put all the SQUARE shapes, like this one, in this
pile." Continue, making one pile each for circles, squares, triangles,
and rectangles. Size and color do not matter.

Note: At this point the child may not yet know the names
of the shapes, but by using the words SAME, DIFFER-
ENT, CIRCLE, SQUARE, TRIANGLE, and RECTANGLE,
you will help him learn.

(34F) IDENTIFYING SHAPES

Place the shapes in the container. Say, "Can you find a REC-
TANGLE in the bowl?" Continue with all the shapes until the container
is empty.

Note: Another way to play this game is to pick out a
piece and ask the child what shape it is.

34G   SHAPES AND COLORS

Place the shapes in the container. Say, "Can you find a BLUE
TRIANGLE in the bowl?" Continue to ask for colored shapes until the
container is empty.

34H   MATCHING SIZES

Place the shapes in the container. Take out one shape and say,
"Can you find another SMALL shape?" (The correct response is to pick
out any other small shape. A small circle can match a small square,
small triangle, or other small shape.) Let the child make a pile of the
pieces he matches correctly. Continue until all of the small and large
shapes have been matched.

> Note: If the child has difficulty, play the game by let-
> ting him pick out the first piece. You match the size.
> Before starting the game, show him that there are two
> sizes of each shape—small and large.

34I   SORTING SIZES

Place all the shapes on the table. Take out any small shape and
say, "Let's put all the SMALL shapes in this pile." Continue, making
one pile each for large and small pieces. Color and shape do not matter.

34J   IDENTIFYING SIZES

Place the shapes in the container. Say, "Can you find a SMALL
shape in the bowl?" Continue with all the pieces until the container is
empty.

34K   SHAPES, COLORS, AND SIZES

Place the shapes in the container. Say, "Can you find a SMALL
BLUE TRIANGLE in the bowl?" Continue to ask for small and large colored shapes until the container is empty.

35 PICKING, PASTING, AND COLORING

Materials: Colored shapes from Activity 34, plain white paper, paste, crayons or magic markers.

Preparation: Trace two of each of the following on plain white paper: four basic shapes (square, rectangle, triangle, circle) in two sizes each —a total of 16. Match the sizes to the cutouts from Activity 34.

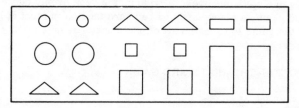

Skills: Understanding colors, shapes, sizes; pasting; crayoning; coordination.

Words to use: Square, circle, triangle, rectangle; large, small; blue, red, yellow; same, different; match.

Place the colored shapes in a pile on the table. Point to the first small circle outline on the white paper and say, "Can you find a SMALL CIRCLE in the pile to MATCH this one?" When a child finds it, he pastes the colored shape over the outline on the white paper.

Now place blue, red, and yellow crayons in front of the child and say, "Can you pick out a RED crayon to MATCH the RED CIRCLE you pasted on the paper?" When the child picks the right crayon, he may color in the circle next to the one he has pasted. Continue in this manner until the paper is filled.

36 MATCH-THE-COLOR CARD GAME

Materials: Deck of playing cards.

Skills: Matching colors.

Words to use: Red, black; same, different; match.

1. Take one black card and one red card from the deck and place them face up on the table. Place the rest of the deck face down on the

table. Turn up the first card and say, "I'm going to MATCH this BLACK card with the one on the table. It belongs in this pile." (Place it on top of the other black card, face up.)

Now ask the child to turn up a card. Say, "On which pile should you put the RED (BLACK) card you picked up?" Continue taking turns picking up cards and placing them in the proper piles.

2. Once the children know BLACK from RED, two or more can play this game by themselves. Divide up the deck evenly between them. Each child places a black card and red card face up in front of him. The object of the game is to match all of one's cards as quickly as possible.

(37) MATCH-THE-SUIT CARD GAME

Materials: Deck of playing cards.

Skills: Matching suits.

Words to use: Hearts, diamonds, clubs, spades; same, different; match.

1. Take one card of each suit from the deck and place them face up on the table. Place the rest of the deck face down on the table. Turn up the first card and say, "I'm going to MATCH this HEART with the one that is the SAME on the table. It belongs in this pile." Place it on top of the other heart, face up.

Now ask the child to turn up a card. Say, "In which pile should you put the SPADE you picked up? Which card has the SAME shapes on it that yours has?" Continue taking turns picking up cards and placing them in the proper piles.

2. Once the children recognize the suits, two or more can play this game by themselves. Divide up the deck evenly between them. Each child places a card of each suit face up in front of him. The object of the game is to match all of one's cards as quickly as possible.

III
Physical Games

Similarly to table games (see p. 21), physical games teach the child impulse control, self-confidence, and good sportsmanship. In addition, they teach coordination. Basic physical coordination and large-muscle development are essential to a child who is to be well prepared for elementary school. Unless handicapped, most children will enjoy running, climbing, hopping, skipping, and other physical activities. Encourage them in all these activities.

(38) PARTS OF THE BODY GAME

Skills: Coordination, naming parts of body, understanding RIGHT and LEFT, following directions.

Words to use: Right, left.

Note: This is a good group game.

1. Everyone stands in a circle. Start with simple commands: "Touch your ear," "Touch your feet," and the like.
When the children have learned to touch the proper part of the body quickly, make your commands harder: "Touch your LEFT foot," "Touch your RIGHT ear with your LEFT hand," and so on. (To make it easier for a child to learn RIGHT and LEFT, tie a ribbon on his right wrist. Then say, "Raise your RIGHT hand—the one with the ribbon on it.")

2. Once the children have learned the game, let them take turns calling the commands.

(39) JACK IN THE BOX

Materials: A large box big enough for a child to sit in.

Skills: Understanding JUMP UP and SIT DOWN.

Words to use: Jump up, sit down.

Place the box in the middle of the floor and ask the child to SIT DOWN in it. Then ask him to JUMP UP.

Sing the song "Pop Goes the Weasel" once through. Explain to the child that the next time you sing it he is to jump up when he hears the word POP. (If you don't know this song, a similar one will do.) If several children are playing, have them all sing the song while they take turns being the jack in the box.

(40) BOX GAME

Materials: A large box or carton, scissors or knife for cutting holes in the box.

Preparation: Cut off the top of the box. Cut two large holes in opposite sides of the box big enough for the child to crawl through.

Skills: Following directions, understanding position and direction.

Words to use: Through, over, into, out, around, in front of, behind, beside.

1. Place the box in the center of the floor and say, "Let's see if you can go INTO the box. " The child will probably be able to do this without help. When he is in the box, you can say, "Let's see you come OUT of the box. "
After he follows these simple directions, add harder ones: "Let's see you crawl THROUGH the box, AROUND the box, " and so on. If he doesn't understand a direction, demonstrate it.

2. Let the children take turns following directions. Once they learn the various words, let them take turns giving directions.

(41) EXERCISE ACTIVITIES

Materials: Record player, phonograph records of music with a beat.

Skills: Developing large muscles; coordination; counting; understanding direction—UP, DOWN, and so on.

Note: These activities are good for the whole class or for a group of children to do together.

1. <u>Exercise to music:</u> Play a music record and do simple exercises to the beat. In a group, the children take turns choosing the next exercise and leading the rest of the group.

2. <u>Simon Says:</u> This is an old game which children still enjoy. The leader gives orders such as: "Simon says touch your toes." Whenever the leader says, "Simon says" do something, the group must do it. If the leader says, "Touch your toes" without first saying "Simon says," the group must <u>not</u> do it. The person who moves when the leader does not say "Simon says," is out. The last one left becomes the new leader.

3. <u>Directions:</u> Say to the child or group of children, "Let's reach way UP." Demonstrate as you say it. Then, "Let's reach way DOWN." Continue reaching in different directions with arms and legs, naming the direction as you do it. Let the children take turns giving the directions.

4. <u>Animal walking:</u> Say, "Let's be ducks," and get into a squat with your hands on your hips and waddle along. Try acting out the walks of various animals. Let the children choose animals too and make up the way they think these animals walk.

(42) BALANCE BOARD AND BALANCE LINE

<u>Materials:</u> A long piece of wood about 1 in. thick and 4 in. wide.

<u>Skills:</u> Balance, coordination.

1. Place the board on the floor or the ground (be sure it is stable and will not tip when walked on). Let the child walk on it, wide side up.

2. For variation, have him try walking backwards.

3. With several children, let them play "Follow the Leader."

4. Instead of a board, use a long piece of string or a strip of paper.

(43) LADDER GAME

<u>Materials:</u> Masking tape, chalk, or paper and scissors; or real ladder.

<u>Preparation:</u> Make a ladder on the floor with masking tape, or outdoors with chalk, or use a real ladder which you place flat on the floor or ground. To make one out of paper, cut strips and paste them together.

<u>Skills:</u> Balance, large-muscle development, coordination.

1. The child walks between the rungs without stepping on the rungs.

2. With several children playing, anyone who touches a rung is out, and the last one left wins.

3. A variation is to walk on the rungs instead of between them.

44 FOLLOW-MY-DIRECTIONS GAME

Skills: Following directions, large-muscle development.

Words to use: Go, walk, crawl, sit, stand, run, over, under, to, through, behind, forward, backward, end, beginning, front, back.

1. Give the child directions to follow, for instance: "CRAWL UNDER the table. SIT on the floor. RUN BEHIND the desk."

2. Several children try to follow the directions as quickly as possible. They can then take turns being leader and giving directions.

3. This game can be played in the "Simon Says" form as well. See Activity 41 for directions.

45 MUSIC ACTIVITIES

Materials: Record player, phonograph records of music with various tempos and rhythms.

Skills: Listening; understanding BEAT; understanding LOUD and SOFT, FAST and SLOW.

Words to use: Loud, soft; fast, slow; beat.

Note: These activities are good for the whole class or for a group of children to do together.

Children take naturally to music. Play phonograph records of music with various tempos and encourage the children to dance and to move about freely to the rhythm of the music. Play a march record and let them march to it. Vary the activity with hopping, skipping, or jumping to the beat.

Vary the volume on your phonograph and talk about LOUD and SOFT. Play music of various tempos and talk about FAST and SLOW beats. Let the children clap or use sticks to keep time with the beat of the music.

Teach the children simple songs and let them make up words to tunes they already know. Singing a song while cleaning up after an art project will make this activity that much more enjoyable.

See Materials, Equipment, and Teaching Aids in the Appendix for ideas on how to make simple children's instruments. Group several children together to form a band.

46 MUSICAL COLORS GAME

Materials: Ten pieces of construction paper, each of a different color and about $8\frac{1}{2}$ in. x 11 in. in size; record player (optional).

Skills: Recognizing colors, appreciating music, developing attention.

Words to use: Blue, red, yellow, and other colors.

Note: This game is to be played by five to ten children.

Place ten pieces of colored paper in a row on the floor, not too close together. Start some music, either by playing a record or singing. When the music starts, the children walk in a circle around the row of colored papers. After a short while, stop the music. As soon as the music stops, each child tries to stand on the paper nearest him.

Start out by having the same number of pieces of paper as children, or a few extra. After the first time the music stops, remove one color and say, "Let's take YELLOW away now." Eventually one child will be left without a paper to stand on, since only one child is allowed to a paper. This child is out. Before you remove another paper, say, "What color should we take away this time? RED? Okay."

One by one the papers are removed and the children are counted out until only one child is left. He is the winner.

47 MARBLES GAME

Materials: Bag of marbles; chalk or masking tape.

Preparation: If playing outside on dirt, dig a shallow hole and mark a line with a stick a few feet back from the hole. On the pavement, draw the circle and line with chalk. If playing inside, use masking tape to form the circle and line on the floor.

Skills: Coordination, concentration.

1. The child kneels behind the line and tries to shoot (roll) the marbles into the circle.

2. If several children are playing, have them take turns shooting their marbles into the circle. The object of the game is to get all of one's marbles into the circle as quickly as possible.

3. Vary the game by having the children try to hit other marbles in the circle and knock them out.

48 BALL IN THE BASKET

Materials: Several balls, a box or basket.

Skills: Coordination, understanding relative size.

Words to use: Small, large; smaller, larger; smallest, largest.

1. The child stands fairly close to the box or basket. Begin with a large ball. The child tries to throw the ball into the basket. As the child gets better at this, have him stand further back.

2. Bring in balls of different sizes. Line up the balls. Talk about the sizes. Say, "Let's see you throw the SMALLEST ball into the basket."

3. If two or more children are playing, each child gets three throws. The object of the game is to get as many balls in the basket as possible.

49 CIRCLE GAMES WITH COLORS AND DIRECTION

Materials: An old sheet or brown paper or cardboard piece measuring 6 ft. x 6 ft.; crayons, paint, or chalk; eight 3 in. x 5 in. index cards or sixteen $1\frac{1}{2}$ in. x $2\frac{1}{2}$ in. cards of thin cardboard or heavy paper.

Preparation: Make a circle about 6 ft. in diameter out of an old sheet, or out of paper or cardboard. Mark, color, and label as shown in the illustration. (The circle can be drawn with chalk on pavement, if you prefer.) Cut eight 3 in. x 5 in. index cards in half, or use thin cardboard or heavy paper to cut sixteen pieces about $1\frac{1}{2}$ in. x $2\frac{1}{2}$ in. Make two cards for each of the eight colors in the circle, crayoning or painting a small circle or patch of color on each card. On one of the two cards draw an arrow pointing to the left. On the other card of the same color draw an arrow pointing to the right. Write the name of the color on each card as shown. (The circle and cards will be used again for Activities 57 and 73.)

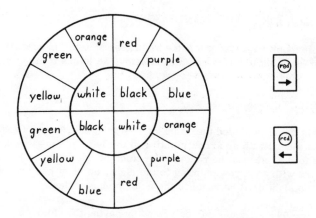

Skills: Crawling, walking, running, hopping, jumping, walking tiptoe, skipping; matching colors; identifying colors; following directions; understanding LEFT and RIGHT.

Words to use: Red, green, blue, and so on; hop, skip, jump, and the like; right, left.

> Note: These games require a lot of room and are best played by a group.

(49A) COLOR MATCH

Place the large circle on the floor or outdoors on the ground. Mix up all the small color cards and place them in a pile face down in the center of the circle.

The first child stands in a white space on the circle and picks the top card. If he picks a green card, he must jump to a green space on the circle. If he picks a yellow card, he must jump to a yellow space, and so on.

The next child stands in the white space, picks a card, and jumps accordingly. Each child stays on the spot he has last jumped to until his turn comes up again. At that time he picks another card and jumps again. If another child is on the color he picked, the player picks another card.

COLOR IDENTIFICATION

This game is played the same as "Color Match," except that the child must say what color he has picked before he jumps to it.

 DIRECTION

This game is played the same as "Color Match," except that if the child picks a card with an arrow pointing to the left, he must hop around the circle to the left until he reaches the color he has picked. If the child picks a card with an arrow pointing to the right, he must hop around the circle to the right until he reaches the color he has picked.

> Note: These games can be varied by having the children skip, crawl, walk, run, walk tiptoe, and so on, as well as hop and jump.

50 ROLE-PLAYING

Materials: As needed for each situation. A prop box or bag with old scarves, hats, shoes, and other clothing is very useful.

Skills: Listening, imitating, developing imagination.

Role-playing is an activity children love. You will find many children doing some of the activities listed below on their own initiative.

1. Pretending to be an animal: Most children think of this activity on their own after watching an animal. They will get down on hands and knees and growl or purr or bark. Encourage them by playing along with them. You might suggest new animals for them to imitate, or take them to a zoo to get some ideas.

2. Teacher-child role switch: It will be a great delight for a child to be the "teacher" while you play the "child." This is a good opportunity for you to hear how the child thinks a teacher does act or should act.

3. Being other people: Pretending to be a doctor, nurse, policeman, policewoman, cowhand, or astronaut is another favorite activity. A few props such as a cowhand's hat, old purse, or stick thermometer will add to the fun. But a child's imagination will go a long way without a doctor's kit or astronaut's uniform being necessary.

4. Dress-up: Bring in some old clothes, hats, and shoes for special dress-up times for the children. Let them put on a parade for other classes.

5. Acting out: Take a child's favorite story and act it out with him. If you have a record of the story, do it in pantomime while listening to it. Let several children take different parts.

6. Hand puppets: Make a hand puppet (see Activity 103) and let the child make up stories or act out one he already knows. Several children can play together.

IV
Number and Letter Activities

The number and letter games are included only for those children who are ready for and interested in them. It may take a long time for a child to become familiar with letters and numbers. Begin with the first activities in each section; they are designed to get the child used to seeing letter and number shapes and learning their names. Proceed with the more difficult activities only if the child shows interest. Play them for short periods of time and do not introduce too many new letters or numbers at a time.

Do not worry if a child does not get to the marked (*) activities before he reaches elementary school age. Children are ready for these skills at different ages, and will certainly be exposed to them again when they enter school. Reading readiness entails more than learning letters. The table games and physical activities provide many of the skills that will prepare the child for reading and writing later on.

Another good preparation for reading is developing a love of books. Read to the children often and give them a chance to tell you about the stories they know. Most preschool children love to have stories read to them. Keep the children interested by changing the tone of your voice as you read and by discussing the story and pictures. Children like to hear the same story over and over again. Soon many children in your class will be able to tell you the story by merely looking at the pictures on the page to refresh their memory.

Teach the young child to respect books. They should not be torn or written in or folded or thrown about. Keep a handy shelf for storing the children's books. Teach the child that books are friends and should be treated with care and respect.

Learning does not occur in even steps. A child may not seem to advance in a particular area for months and then all of a sudden may pick up many new learnings in a week's time. Therefore, if a child cannot do a particular activity, put it aside for the time being. Continue to enrich and expand his experiences in other areas. Then at a later time try again. If the opportunity is available, he will reach out when he is ready.

NUMBER ACTIVITIES

⑤¹ NUMBER TREE

<u>Materials:</u> Construction paper, scissors, paste, white paper, pencil, crayons or magic markers.

<u>Preparation:</u> Draw the numbers 1 through 9 several times on colored paper and cut them out. The shapes should be large enough for easy pasting.

<u>Skills:</u> Becoming familiar with numbers.

<u>Words to use:</u> One, two, three, and so on.

Say, "Let's make a number tree. First we'll draw the trunk and branches." Show the child how to do it. (See illustration.)

Say, "Now that we have the trunk and branches, we can put the numbers on." Spread the colored numbers on the table in front of the child. Show the child how to put paste on one side of the number and place it on a branch of the tree. As you paste, talk about the number. Mention its name. For example: "What number would you like to paste on first? This one? That's number FOUR. Where do you want to paste number FOUR?" Let the child continue pasting numbers on the tree until he is satisfied that it is full enough.

> Note: This project can be hung on the wall, providing opportunities in the future to talk about the numbers again. The basic purpose of the project is for the child to become used to seeing the numbers and hearing their names.

52 NUMBER MOBILE

Materials: A stick, string, construction paper, scissors, paste or hole punch.

Preparation: Make numbers as described in the Preparation for Activity 51.

Skills: Becoming familiar with numbers.

Words to use: One, two, three, and so on.

Tie several strings to hang down from the stick as shown in the illustration.

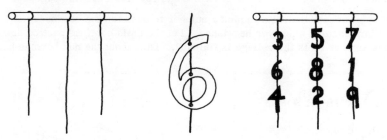

Say, "We are going to make a number mobile to hang in the room. Pick out a number you like and we'll paste it to this string." Have the child pick a number. Show the child how to put paste on the number and glue it to the string.

Another method is to make a hole with a hole punch at each end of the number and thread the string through.

The child continues to pick out numbers to put on the mobile. Each time he picks one, call it by name: "Oh, now you've got number FIVE. Where are you going to put number FIVE?"

When the mobile is completely dry, hang it from the ceiling in the classroom.

53 NUMBER COLLAGE

Materials: Construction paper; paste; scissors; large piece of cardboard or heavy paper; old magazine pages, cloth, tissue paper, and other materials.

Preparation: Cut out the numbers 1 through 9 from a variety of materials. The shapes should be large enough for easy pasting.

Skills: Becoming familiar with numbers.

Words to use: One, two, three, and so on; collage.

Place a large piece of cardboard or heavy paper in front of the child and the numbers in a pile near him. Say, "Let's make a COLLAGE. That's a picture made of different kinds of materials. See all these numbers? Feel them. What are they made of?"

While the child is exploring the different materials of the numbers, talk to him about them, naming the numbers he touches: "That one feels smooth, doesn't it? That's a THREE made out of a magazine page."

Now ask the child to pick a number to paste on the cardboard. Let him paste it wherever he wishes. Let the child continue pasting numbers until he feels the collage is finished. Talk about the numbers as he pastes them.

54 NUMBER SONGS

Skills: Counting.

Words to use: One, two, three, and so on.

To encourage children to count, teach them songs with numbers in them, such as "One, Two, Buckle My Shoe." Make up your own songs with numbers. An example:

> This is my number ONE finger—so tiny and so small.
> This is my number TWO finger—a little bigger, that's all.
> This is my number THREE finger—it's biggest and in the middle.
> This is my number FOUR finger—we step from big to little.
> This is my number FIVE finger—ooops, I mean thumb!

Show the child how to count his toes, fingers, and steps, or objects such as crayons or building blocks.

55 GIANT STEP

Skills: Listening, counting, following directions.

Words to use: One, two, three, and so on; giant, baby.

Note: This game is to be played by four or more children.

The leader stands at one end of the room. The rest of the children stand at the other end. The object of the game is to take enough steps to reach the leader.

The first child says to the leader, "May I take ONE (TWO, THREE) GIANT step?" The leader answers, "Yes, you may," OR "No, you may take ONE BABY step," OR "No, you may take TWO GIANT steps," OR some similar response. The child takes as many small (baby) or large (giant) steps as the leader tells him to. Then the next child asks to take some steps.

The game continues until one child reaches the leader. He is the winner and becomes the new leader.

56 LET'S COUNT

Materials: Any available objects, several of a kind; a bag or bowl to hold the objects.

Skills: Counting.

Words to use: One, two, three, and so on.

1. Say, "Let's count apples (stones, nuts, pencils). I've got ONE apple (take one apple from a bag or bowl). Now it's your turn. You take an apple. How many do you have?" After the child says he has one apple, continue: "I've got TWO apples now (take another one)." The child takes another apple and tells you how many he has now.

2. Play this game with different objects in the classroom at different times. When the child is interested, let him try to go first. He may not count perfectly at first, but with your help he will become better at it.

57 CIRCLE GAMES WITH NUMBERS

Materials: The large circle and cards from Activity 49.

Preparation: Using the large circle from Activity 49, print any number from 1 to 9 in each of the twelve outer sections. The numbers do not have to be in order. Then on each card print any number from 1 to 9 below the arrow. Now the circle and cards can be used for the "Circle Games with Numbers" as well as for "Colors" and "Direction."

Skills: Crawling, walking, running, hopping, jumping, walking tiptoe, skipping; matching numbers; identifying numbers.

Words to use: One, two, three, and so on; hop, skip, and the like.

Note: These games require a lot of room and are best played by a group.

 NUMBER MATCH

Place the large circle on the floor or outdoors on the ground. Mix up all the cards and place them in a pile face down in the center of the circle.

The first child stands in a white space on the circle and picks the top card. If he picks a number five card, he must jump to a number five space on the circle. If he picks a number two card, he must jump to a number two space.

The next child stands in the white space, picks a card, and jumps accordingly. Each child stays on the spot he has last jumped to until his turn comes up again. At that time he picks another card and jumps again.

57B NUMBER IDENTIFICATION

This game is played the same as "Number Match" (57A), except that the child must say what number he has picked before he jumps to it.

Note: These games can be varied by having the children skip, crawl, walk, run, walk tiptoe, and so on, as well as jump and hop.

58 SPIN-THE-BOTTLE NUMBER GAME

Materials: Narrow-necked bottle; large piece of paper, cardboard, or fabric; crayons or magic markers; scissors; plain paper.

Preparation: Cut a large circle out of cardboard, paper, or fabric such as burlap. Mark it off into ten sections. Print a different number from 0 to 9 in each section. Print the number right side up and upside down so it can be seen from both sides. Cut up paper into forty 2 in. x 1 in. pieces. Print each number from 0 to 9 on four cards.

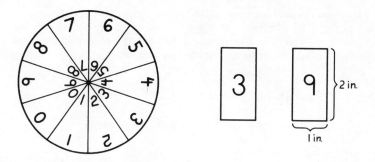

Skills: Matching numbers, waiting one's turn.

Note: This game is to be played by two or more children.

Place the circle on the table or floor in the center of all players. Mix up the cards and divide them equally among the players.

The first player spins the bottle in the center of the circle. When it stops spinning, the neck of the bottle will end up in a numbered space. If the player has a card with this number on it, he places it on the appropriate wedge in the circle. The next player does the same. If a player does not have the number he lands on, the next player has his turn. The object of the game is to use up one's cards as fast as possible.

(59) MATCH-THE-NUMBER CARD GAME

Materials: Deck of playing cards without picture cards and aces.

Skills: Matching numbers.

Words to use: Two, three, four, five, six, seven, eight, nine, ten; same, different; match.

1. Take one card of each number and place them face up on the table. Place the rest of the deck face down on the table. Turn up the first card and say, "I'm going to MATCH this THREE with the THREE on the table. It belongs in this pile." Place it on top of the other three on the table, face up.

Now ask the child to turn up a card. Say, "In which pile should you put the FOUR you picked up? Which number here is the SAME as the FOUR you have?" (It is not necessary for the child to be able to read and name the numbers. Merely try to see if he can match the cards correctly.) Continue taking turns picking up cards and placing them in the proper piles.

2. Once the children recognize the numbers, two or more can play this game by themselves. Divide up the deck evenly between them, leaving one of each number face up on the table. The object of the game is to match all of one's cards as quickly as possible.

*(60) IDENTIFY-THE-CARD GAME

Materials: Deck of playing cards without pictures or aces.

Skills: Identifying numbers.

Words to use: Two, three, four, and so on.

1. Mix up the cards and place them face down on the table. (You may wish to start with only the low numbers at first to make it easier for the child.)
Ask the child to turn over the first card. If he can identify the card by naming its number, he puts it in his own pile. If the child does not identify a card properly, tell him what the number is and put the card in another pile. The child continues turning over the cards and identifying them, trying to get as many cards in his pile as possible.

2. To play this game with a group of children, let them take turns turning over a card and naming it. If a child names the number correctly, he puts the card in his own pile. If he is wrong, he puts the card back on the bottom of the deck.

*(61) MATCH THE NUMBER

Materials: Large sheet of paper; crayon, pen, or magic marker.

Preparation: On a large sheet of paper, draw sets of one, two, and three circles at the left and the numbers 1, 2, and 3 at the right. The numbers and the sets of circles should not match across the page.

```
┌─────────────────────────────┐
│                             │
│   O O O          1          │
│                             │
│   O O            3          │
│                             │
│   O              2          │
│                             │
└─────────────────────────────┘
```

Skills: Identifying numbers, understanding what the numbers mean, understanding sets.

Words to use: One, two, three; set.

    1. Point to the number 1 and say, "Do you know what number this is?" After the child answers, say, "Let's find ONE circle to match it with. We will call this circle a SET of ONE." When the child points to the single circle, have him draw a line from the number 1 to the single circle.
    Repeat with numbers 2 and 3. Use the word SET: "Let's draw a line from the number TWO to this SET of TWO circles."

    2. When the child can do this activity easily with numbers 1, 2, and 3, try it with larger numbers.

*(62) NUMBER-SHAPE ACTIVITY

Materials: Large sheet of white paper, crayons, colored construction paper, scissors, paste.

Preparation: Following the patterns in the illustration, draw outlines of the shapes on a large sheet of white paper. Print the numbers in crayon on the left-hand side of the sheet. Out of colored construction paper, cut enough pieces of each shape for the child to paste over the outlines, that is, one large rectangle, two large squares, three triangles, and so on.

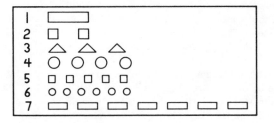

Skills: Identifying shapes, understanding the meaning of numbers, counting, coordination.

Words to use: Rectangle, triangle, circle, square; large, small; one, two, three, and so on.

    1. Place the colored shapes on the table. Point to the first large rectangle outline on the paper and say, "Can you find ONE LARGE RECTANGLE in the pile to paste on this one?" Next, point to the two large

square outlines and say, "Can you find TWO LARGE SQUARES to paste on these?"

Continue in the same manner using the words ONE, TWO, THREE, FOUR, and so on. Let the child paste the shapes as he finds them. After the paper is filled, count each line again with the child. Point to the numbers as you count.

2. Once the paper is filled and the child is familiar with the numbers, point to a line and ask him to tell you how many shapes there are in it: "How many LARGE TRIANGLES are there in this line?" If the child cannot answer correctly, help him count the shapes again.

3. Hanging this project in the classroom will not only make the child proud of his work, but will help him become familiar with the numbers each time he looks at it.

 PILING CHIPS

Materials: Pile of poker chips (if you don't have any, pennies or anything that stacks easily will do).

Skills: Understanding EQUAL and UNEQUAL, counting, adding 1.

Words to use: Equal, unequal; same, different; amount; one, two, three, and so on; add.

1. Say, "Let's make some stacks of chips." Begin to make small stacks of two, three, or four chips. After the child has made a few stacks, bring two of the same height together and show him that the tops of the stacks are even. "Look, these stacks of chips are the SAME. Do you think they have the SAME AMOUNT of chips in them? Let's count and see."

Show the child that each stack has three chips in it by taking the chips off one by one. "See, they each have THREE chips. Now let's put them back into stacks." After the child puts them back, say, "See, the stacks are still the SAME. They are EQUAL because they both have THREE chips."

Try this procedure on other stacks, some equal and some unequal. Let the child count the chips himself if he can.

2. Point to two even stacks and ask, "Are these two piles EQUAL or UNEQUAL?"

3. Make a stack of two chips and let the child count the chips by taking them off one by one. Ask him to stack them again. Now have him add one chip. Let him recount the chips again. He will see that the stack now has three chips. Let him try this procedure a few times until he sees that adding one more chip brings the stack to the next higher number.

(64) CARD GAMES

Materials: Deck of playing cards (you may wish to take out all the aces and picture cards in order not to confuse the child).

Skills: Identifying numbers, understanding which number is higher or lower.

> Note: These games are to be played by two or more players.

(64A) WAR

Deal out all cards equally to all players. Each player places one card face up in the center of the table. The player who has the highest-numbered card wins all the cards that are up. If two or more players put out the same number, each of these players places three more cards face down and one up. The player with the highest card up takes all the cards played. The game is over when one person has all the cards. Or set a time limit, and the player who has the most cards at that time wins.

(64B) RUMMY

Deal each player seven cards. Place the rest face down on the table. Turn the top card up and place it face up next to the pile. The first player has the choice of picking up this card or the top card from the other pile. The object is to get three or four cards with the same number. Each time a card is picked up, the player must put one down from his hand in the face-up pile. Whenever a player gets three cards of one number, he puts them in a pile face up on the table. Any player can add a fourth card to any pile on the table. The object of the game is to get rid of all the cards in one's hand.

*(65) MEASURING ACTIVITIES

Materials: Ruler, yardstick, tape measure, measuring cups, quart containers, and other measuring equipment.

Skills: Understanding measurement and distance, counting.

Words to use: Inch, foot, yard; long, length, height; cup, pint, quart, gallon; half, quarter. (Meter, liter, gram, and so on.)

1. Child's height: Children are interested in themselves and their own growth. A good way to introduce measurement is to have the

child measure himself. Let him stand against a wall. Place a mark at the top of his head. (If you don't want to mark the wall, paste a piece of paper on the wall first.) Let the child take a 12-inch or foot ruler and measure the distance, in feet and inches, from the floor to the mark.

2. Classroom: Once the child is familiar with the use of a ruler, he can measure the classroom next. Perhaps here you can show him how to use a yardstick or tape measure. Later he may discover how the foot ruler fits on the yardstick three times because there are three feet in a yard. Help him count the 12 inches on the ruler to see that this distance makes one foot.

3. Liquid measure: Let the child fill a measuring cup with water and pour it into an empty one-quart milk carton to discover that it takes four cups full of water to make a quart. If you have a pint carton, use this next. Also use half-cup measures, half-gallon cartons, and gallon and other measures.

*(66) MONEY ACTIVITIES

Materials: Pennies, nickels, dimes, quarters, pencil, paper.

Skills: Counting, understanding money values, understanding EQUAL.

Words to use: Penny, nickel, dime, quarter; equal; one, two, three, and so on.

1. Start by having the child count pennies. Let him count five pennies and put them in a stack. Say, "Did you know that it takes FIVE PENNIES to make ONE NICKEL? FIVE PENNIES EQUAL ONE NICKEL. Let's make a drawing of this." On a piece of paper, print an equal sign (=) in the middle. Have the child trace five pennies on the left of the equal sign and a nickel on the right.

Ask the child to count ten pennies and stack them in a pile. Tell him this equals one dime. Let him trace these on paper in the same manner as above.

Continue with "two nickels equal one dime," "two dimes and one nickel equal one quarter," and so on. Go slowly. You may only get as far as "one nickel equals five pennies" in the first few sessions.

2. When the tracing is finished, say, "Let's do some trading now. If I give you ONE NICKEL, how many PENNIES should you give me in return?" Let the child look at the paper to see how many pennies equal one nickel.

* (67)   TRACE THE NUMBER, PRINT THE NUMBER

Materials: Blackboard and colored chalk; or paper, pencil, and crayons or magic markers.

Skills: Learning to form numbers.

Words to use: Trace; one, two, three, and so on.

> Note: Tracing and printing numbers may be introduced after the child has learned to recognize the numbers from 1 to 10, can count from 1 to 10, and has a clear understanding of what the numbers mean.

1. On a blackboard (or piece of paper) print the number 1 very large and clear. Say, "Would you like to trace this number 1? Take your finger and follow the line like this." Show the child how to trace over it with his finger. Say, "Now you can take the chalk (pencil) and trace over the number 1." It will be more fun for the child if he can trace with a different-colored chalk, crayon, or magic marker. Do the same with another easy number to print, such as 7. Continue with other numbers as long as the child shows interest.

2. On a blackboard (or piece of paper) print the number 1 very large and clear. Next to it, ask the child to draw a copy of your 1. Praise all his first efforts. Do not expect the line to be straight. Now go on to another easy number, such as 7. Let him print just 7s and 1s for a while until he can do them easily and is ready to try another number.

LETTER ACTIVITIES

(68)   LETTER TREE

Materials: Construction paper, scissors, paste, white paper, pencil, crayons or magic markers.

Preparation: Draw all the letters of the alphabet on colored construction paper and cut them out. The shapes should be large enough for easy pasting. Use either uppercase or lowercase letters.

Skills: Becoming familiar with letters.

Words to use: A, b, c, and so on.

Say, "Let's make a letter tree. First we'll draw the trunk and branches." Show the child how to do it. (See comparable Activity 51.)

Say, "Now that we have the trunk and branches, we can put the letters on." Spread the colored letters in front of the child. Show the child how to put paste on one side of the letter and place it on a branch of the tree. As you paste, talk about the letter. Mention its name. For example: "What letter would you like to paste on first? This one? That's the letter C. Where do you want to paste the letter C?" Let the child continue pasting letters on the tree until he is satisfied that it is full enough.

Note: This project can be hung on the wall, providing opportunities in the future to talk about the letters again.

 LETTER MOBILE

Materials: A stick, string, construction paper, scissors, paste or hole punch.

Preparation: Make letters as described in the Preparation for Activity 68.

Skills: Becoming familiar with letters.

Words to use: A, b, c, and so on.

Tie several strings to hang down from the stick. (See comparable Activity 52.)

Say, "We are going to make a letter mobile to hang in the room. Pick out a letter you like and we'll paste it to this string." Have the child pick a letter. Show the child how to put paste on the letter and glue it to the string.

Another method is to make a hole with a hole punch at each end of the letter and thread the string through.

The child continues to pick out letters to put on the mobile. Each time he picks one, call it by name: "Oh, now you've got the letter E. Where are you going to put the E?"

When the mobile is completely dry, hang it from the ceiling in the classroom.

(70) LETTER COLLAGE

Materials: Construction paper; paste; scissors; large piece of cardboard or heavy paper; old magazines, tissue paper, cloth, and other materials.

Preparation: Using construction paper, magazine pages, cloth, tissue paper, and other materials, cut out letters as described in the Preparation for Activity 68.

Skills: Becoming familiar with letters.

Words to use: Capital a, b, c; small a, b, c; and so on; collage.

Place a large piece of cardboard or heavy paper in front of the child and the letters in a pile near him. Say, "Let's make a COLLAGE. That's a picture made of different kinds of materials. See all these letters? Feel them. How do they feel?"

While the child is exploring the different materials of the letters, talk to him about them, naming the letters as he touches them: "That one feels smooth, doesn't it? That's a SMALL B made out of a magazine page."

Now ask the child to pick a letter to paste on the cardboard. Let him paste it wherever he wishes. Let the child continue pasting letters until he feels that the collage is finished. Talk about the letters as he pastes them.

(71) LABELING

Materials: Cards or small pieces of cardboard or paper approximately 2 in. in width; pen, crayon, or magic marker; thumbtacks or masking tape (masking tape will come off painted surfaces more easily than transparent tape, which is likely to pull off paint).

Skills: Becoming familiar with words; recognizing one's name.

1. On a piece of cardboard or paper, print the child's name in clear uppercase and lowercase letters. If the child can recognize the letters, have him spell the word out loud. Otherwise point to each letter and say it for him. Then say, "We will put your name tag on your chair to show that it is your chair." Tape or tack the cardboard on the child's chair or near his coat hook.

2. Make tags for various items in the room, such as chair, table, door, and floor. Let the child help you tape them on each item. Refer to these words often. By constantly seeing them, the child will become familiar with them. Do not make too many labels so as not to confuse the child. Start out with a few simple ones and add more later.

 STOP-THE-MUSIC LETTER GAME

Materials: Twenty-six pieces of paper about 8½ in. x 11 in. in size; crayon or magic marker; record player (optional).

Preparation: On each piece of paper print a letter of the alphabet, capital and small side by side.

Skills: Familiarity with letters, developing attention, appreciating music.

Words to use: A, b, c, and so on.

Note: This game is best played by ten or more children.

Place the 26 sheets of paper in one or two rows on the floor, not too close together. Start the music, either by playing a record or singing. When the music starts, the children walk in a circle around the row of papers. After a short while, stop the music. As soon as the music stops, each child tries to stand on the paper nearest him.

After the first time the music stops, remove one paper and say, "Let's take the letter F away now." Eventually one child will be left without a paper to stand on, since only one child is allowed to a paper. This child is out. Before you remove another paper, say, "What letter should we take away now? C? Okay."

One by one the papers are removed and the children are counted out until only one child is left. He is the winner.

73 CIRCLE GAMES WITH LETTERS

Materials: The large circle and cards from Activities 49 and 57.

Preparation: Using the large circle from Activity 49, print a letter in each of the twelve outer sections. Some sections will have two or three letters in them. Then on each card print a letter above the arrow. Now the circle and cards can be used for the "Circle Games with Letters" as well as for "Colors," "Direction," and "Numbers."

Skills: Crawling, walking, running, hopping, jumping, walking tiptoe, skipping; matching letters; identifying letters.

Words to use: A, b, c, and so on; hop, skip, jump, and the like.

> Note: These games require a lot of room and are best played by a group.

(73A) LETTER MATCH

Place the large circle on the floor or outdoors on the ground. Mix up all the cards and place them in a pile face down in the center of the circle.

The first child stands in a white space on the circle and picks the top card. If he picks a letter S card, he must jump to a letter S space on the circle. If he picks a letter Y card, he must jump to a letter Y space.

The next child stands in the white space, picks a card, and jumps accordingly. Each child stays on the spot he has last jumped to until his turn comes up again. At that time he picks another card and jumps again.

(73B) LETTER IDENTIFICATION

This game is played the same as "Letter Match" (73A), except that the child must say what letter he has picked before he jumps to it.

> Note: These games can be varied by having the children skip, crawl, walk, run, walk tiptoe, and so on, as well as jump and hop.

(74) SPIN-THE-BOTTLE LETTER GAME

Materials: Narrow-necked bottle; large piece of paper, cardboard, or fabric; crayons or magic markers; scissors; plain paper.

Preparation: Cut a large circle out of cardboard, paper, burlap, or other material. Mark it off into as many sections (wedges) as possible. Print a letter of the alphabet in each section (some sections may have more than one letter if you run out of space). Cut up paper into fifty-two 2 in. x 1 in. pieces. Print each letter from A to Z, both uppercase and lowercase, on two cards.

Skills: Matching letters, waiting one's turn.

Note: This game is to be played by two or more children.

Place the circle on the table or floor in the center of all players. Mix up the cards and divide them equally among the players.

The first player spins the bottle in the center of the circle. When it stops spinning, the neck of the bottle will end up in a lettered space. If the player has a card with this letter on it, he places that card on the appropriate wedge in the circle. The next player does the same. If a player does not have the letter he lands on, the next player has his turn. The object of the game is to use up one's cards as fast as possible.

*(75) SIGNS AND LABELS GAME

Materials: Cans, boxes, and other items with labels.

Skills: Recognizing letters, recognizing words.

Words to use: Capital letter, small letter.

1. Spread out a number of cans, boxes, and other items with labels. Ask the child to look for certain letters: "Let's find CAPITAL L's on this can."

2. If a child is able to recognize a few simple words, ask him to find these on the labels: TO, AT, IN, and the like.

3. When you take your class for a walk, let the children look for letters on signs they see.

*(76) MATCH-THE-LETTERS GAME

Materials: Oaktag or cardboard, scissors.

Preparation: Outline and cut every letter of the alphabet, both uppercase and lowercase.

Skills: Identifying small and capital letters.

Words to use: Small a, capital a; small b, capital b; and so on.

1. If the child can identify all the capital letters of the alphabet, but still needs to learn to identify the small letters, play the game thus:

Place all the letter cutouts on the table. Pick out a small letter and say,
"This is the SMALL letter F. Can you find the CAPITAL F?" Continue
in this manner until all the letters have been matched.

2. Once the child begins to learn what the small letters look like,
reverse the procedure. Pick out a capital letter and ask him to find the
corresponding small letter.

*(77) COUNT-THE-LETTERS GAME

Materials: Children's storybooks.

Skills: Recognizing letters, counting.

1. Take out a children's storybook and say, "Let's see how many
A's we can find on this page." See if the child can find the first A. If he
can, let him search the rest of the words for more A's, counting them
as he finds them.

2. If the child cannot recognize the first A, point it out to him
and ask him if he sees any more letters like it on the page. Print the
small and capital letters (A a) on a card for his use as a guide. A child
may recognize capital letters before small letters; therefore, make sure
you show him what both forms look like.

3. If the child can recognize the letters but cannot count yet,
count for him as he points to each letter.

*(78) RHYMING GAME

Skills: Rhyming, vocabulary.

Words to use: Same, rhyme.

1. Say to the child, "Say, may, day, play—do these words sound
the SAME? The word SAY RHYMES with DAY, PLAY, and MAY. This
means the ends of the words sound the SAME. LOOK and BOOK both end
with OOK. Can you think of a word that RHYMES with CAT?"
At first the child may have difficulty understanding the concept of
rhyme. In the beginning it might be easier to offer him two choices:
"What word sounds like DO—EAT or TO?"

2. Once several children understand what a rhyme is, you can
make a game out of it. The first player says a word. The second player
says a word which rhymes with it. Each player must say a different word
which rhymes with the first word. If a player cannot think of a rhyming
word, the next player has his turn.

*(79) MY OWN NAME

Materials: Blackboard and colored chalk; or paper, pencil, and crayons or magic markers.

Skills: Learning to form letters, coordination.

Words to use: Trace; a, b, c, and so on.

1. The first word that a child shows interest in learning how to print is usually his own name. First he should learn to recognize it when he sees it printed. Then begin teaching him to trace it.
Start by printing his name, letter by letter, in uppercase and lowercase letters. On the blackboard (or paper) print the capital L (or whatever letter begins the child's name) very large and clear. Say, "Let's see if you can trace this L. Take your finger and go over it like this." Show him how to trace over it with his finger. "Now take the chalk (pencil) and trace over the letter L." It will be more fun for the child if he can trace with a different-colored chalk, crayon, or magic marker. Do the same with the lowercase letters of the name.

2. Next, let the child try to form the letters of his name himself, preferably next to a sample done by you. Praise his early efforts. Don't expect perfection.

*(80) LETTER-SOUND BOOK

Materials: Scrapbook (see Activity 1 Preparation), old magazines, crayons or magic markers, capital and small construction-paper letters (see Activity 68 Preparation), paste.

Preparation: From magazines cut out pictures whose names start with different letters: APPLE, BALL, COW, and so on.

Skills: Understanding letter sounds, matching letters, printing letters.

Say, "Let's make a letter-sound scrapbook. We'll start with A." Print a capital A at the top left-hand corner of the first page. Print the small A beneath it. Say the sound the letter makes.

Say, "Can you find a picture whose name starts with the sound of the letter A?" Go through all the pictures, asking the child what the name of each is. When he reaches APPLE say, "APPLE starts with an A."

Then have the child paste the picture of the apple next to the letters A. Underneath the picture, print the word APPLE.

Ask the child to find the letter A in the pile of cutout letters. When he finds the small and capital letters, let him paste them on the page.

Print the capital A and small A in pencil. Ask the child to trace them with a crayon or magic marker.

Finally, if the child wants to, let him print the A's on the page himself.

Continue in a similar manner through the rest of the alphabet.

Note: Instead of using magazine pictures, you may want to let the child draw or paint a picture of each object.

V
Craft Activities

The following activities provide a basic introduction to the many art and craft forms so popular today. Although we have given specific examples of these activities, please allow the child freedom to experiment.

Before using messy materials, set the limits of their use. Keep in mind that a child given paint for the first time will make a considerable mess if guidelines are not established. It is also essential that an area be set aside where no damage can be done and where the child has relative freedom. It is not fair to allow a child to paint on a wall one time and scold him for doing so the next time. Be fair and firm about the use of the materials, always remembering to be flexible in allowing them to be used in many ways within the limits set by you.

Some children will not use materials such as fingerpaint or clay for fear of getting dirty. Keep in mind that the child has probably been told many times to stay clean and may be afraid to get dirty for fear of upsetting you. Reassure him that it is fine to play with these materials. If the child still refuses, do not force him. Seeing other children use such materials may convince him to try.

Use different sizes, shapes, and textures of paper. Save egg cartons, bottle tops, string, seeds, macaroni, ribbon, buttons, wrapping and tissue paper, old greeting cards, and scraps of material. Make sure that any materials you select are safe for a child to use. Be careful of sharp edges.

As your collection of materials grows, you and the child will find ways to use them beyond the activities mentioned here. Let the child's imagination work to create and explore.

Before beginning any craft activity, especially one that involves liquid materials and messy scraps, prepare the work area and ready the child as follows:

- Protect the floor from spills and dripping with newspapers or plastic around the easel or table.

- Move other furniture out of the way. If necessary, protect furniture with newspaper or plastic coverings.

- Put a smock or apron on the child or have him wear old clothes. An old blouse put on backwards makes a good smock. Roll up his sleeves.

- Pour paint into individual cups or trays and provide easy accessibility to all materials.

Rather than listing separate skills for each activity, we have listed below the basic skills and concepts developed throughout the craft activities:

> manual dexterity
> observing—understanding why and how things happen
> experimenting
> imagination
> self-expression
> creativity
> eye-hand coordination
> sense of balance
> using tools
> memory, concentration, and perseverence
> measuring
> drawing
> classifying
> understanding colors, shapes, sizes, and relationships
> identifying objects and developing vocabulary
> sensitivity to art and beauty
> self-confidence
> problem-solving

You will find that the craft activities are arranged in no particular order of difficulty. The younger child may not paste neatly, or may have difficulty managing scissors. The amount of teacher assistance will depend on the child's ability. Let him do as much as he can himself. It does not matter if the finished product looks imperfect. It is more important that the child gain the experience and pride which come from producing something through his own efforts. He should not be sitting there watching <u>you</u> make something. If you need to do certain things for him, it would be best to do them in advance, or find something else for him to do while you are busy. Recognize his accomplishments and let him tell you about what he has done. Display his work proudly!

 PAINTING

<u>Materials:</u> Any water-base paint such as tempera or poster paint (paint may come in liquid form or in powder to be mixed with water; water paint in hard cakes can also be used successfully and is preferred by some; when painting on a slightly waxy surface, adding a small amount of liquid detergent to the paint will help the paint adhere); paint cups—any small containers, such as juice cans, to hold small amounts of paint; brushes—all

sizes (preferably ½-1 in. wide); large pieces of paper; easel, if available (if you do not have an easel, use a cardboard soda bottle carrier to keep the cans of paint in an upright position; it also facilitates cleanup and storage); bowl or cup of water for cleaning brushes; rag or paper towel; sponge.

Preparation: Assemble all materials. Pour a small amount of each color paint into paint cups.

Words to use: Red, yellow, blue, and so on; light, dark; sponge; brush; easel; wet, dry.

1. Place one large sheet of paper on the easel or table in front of the child and give him two or three primary colors to start with (yellow, red, blue).

Show the child how to dip his brush in the paint and apply it to the paper. Hand him the brush and let him try it. Show the child how to clean out the brush in the water and dry it on a rag or sponge. Explain that cleaning the brush before you dip it in the next color will keep the colors bright and clean. To make it easier for a child who is new to painting, provide a brush for each color so he doesn't have to clean it when changing colors.

Let the child paint until he says the picture is finished. Place it aside to dry. Some children are finished with a picture after a few strokes. Don't expect the child to conform to your idea of what "finished" means.

2. Let the child discover what happens if he mixes yellow and red. Provide empty cups to make mixtures of primary colors. (Red + yellow = orange, red + blue = purple, yellow + blue = green.) Give the child some white paint. Encourage him to mix it with the other colors to let him see how it lightens the other colors. Give the child some black paint to let him see how it darkens the other colors. Let the child experiment with mixing other colors. Do not be upset if he makes only muddy colors or only wants to paint with one color.

3. Call colors by their proper names to encourage the child to learn them.

4. Ask the child, "Tell me about your picture." You may wish to print what he tells you on the picture. Hang his "story-picture" where the whole class can admire it.

5. When the child is finished painting, show him how to clean the brushes thoroughly with soap and water. Let him help you put the caps tightly on the paint and wipe the table or easel clean.

6. In future painting sessions, try paper with different textures. Always use large sheets if possible. Even newspaper can be interesting to paint on.

FINGERPAINTING

Materials: Fingerpaint (see Preparation); fingerpaint paper, or any paper with a shiny surface such as shelving paper; sponge; bowl of water; rag or paper towel.

Preparation: Assemble all materials. Prepare a flat work area. Fingerpaint can be bought, or made with the following recipe: Soften $\frac{1}{2}$ cup of dry starch in a small amount of cold water. Add this to 1 quart of boiling water. Heat and stir until the mixture bubbles. Remove and cool slightly. Add $\frac{1}{2}$ cup soap flakes. Stir until well mixed. Cool. Place in jars. Add tempera or vegetable coloring. Keep in the refrigerator.

Words to use: Fingerpaint, design, push, mix, press, wet, sticky; names of colors.

1. Wet both sides of the paper and place it flat on the table. Place a spoonful of paint on the paper and let the child spread it around. Encourage him to use hands, arms, or objects to make designs, and to experiment with more than one color.

2. Guide the child in the following: Take another sheet of paper and place it on top of the finished picture. Press and remove to make a print of the first painting. Set the finished paintings aside to dry.

83 FINGERPAINT SNOW

Materials: Soap flakes, water, food coloring, egg beater, bowl.

Preparation: Mix two parts soap flakes with one part water. Let the child help you beat the soap flakes and water to a thick consistency. Add food coloring.

Words to use: Fingerpaint snow, soap, thick, creamy; names of colors.

1. Use Fingerpaint Snow the same way you would use regular fingerpaint (see Activity 82).

2. Since Fingerpaint Snow is so clean, you can use it directly on a smooth tabletop if desired. Simply wipe it off when finished.

Note: Remember, soap is slippery, so wipe up spills quickly.

84 SPATTER PAINTING

Materials: Thinned tempera paint or similar liquid paint, old toothbrush, paper of different color than paint, spatter-paint frame (see Preparation), scissors, construction paper, shelving paper.

Preparation: The frame should be 2 in. in depth with screening across the top. You can make a frame from a cigar box by taking out the top and bottom and stapling screening to one side. One can also do this activity without a spatter-paint screen by rubbing a finger or stick across the toothbrush while holding it face down over the paper.

Words to use: Spatter, spots, pattern, design; names of colors.

1. Place the spatter-paint frame on top of a piece of paper. Let the child dip the toothbrush into the paint. Then show him how to rub the toothbrush across the top of the screen, spattering the paper below. Encourage him to use several colors for varying effects.

2. Cut patterns of hearts, circles, squares, and other shapes out of another piece of paper. Place a pattern on top of a clean sheet. Then let the child spatter the sheet. Remove the patterns.

3. Help the child spatter sheets of shelving paper to make gift-wrapping paper, or spatter folded construction paper to make greeting cards.

85 SPONGE PAINTING

Materials: Old sponges, scissors, tempera paint, pans to hold paint (old pie tins or baking pans work well), paper to paint on, water for cleaning sponges, construction paper and shelving paper.

Preparation: Cut the sponges into pieces of various sizes and shapes.

Words to use: Sponge, dip, soak; design, pattern; big, small; thin, fat; names of colors and shapes.

1. Pour a small amount of paint into a tray or pan. Let the child dip a sponge into the paint, then place it on paper and press. The pattern can be repeated several times with one dip of the sponge. The texture of the sponge will show through as more prints are made. Encourage the child to combine several shapes.

Point out to the child how the sponge soaks up the paint. Mention the names of the colors and shapes: BIG shapes and SMALL shapes, THIN shapes and FAT shapes, and so on.

2. Sponge painting can be used to make gift-wrapping paper out of shelving paper or greeting cards from construction paper.

(86) STRING PAINTING

Materials: Several 10-12 in. pieces of string; tempera paint; paper; shallow tray (TV dinner tray, jar-top, or saucer).

Preparation: Pour a small amount of paint into each tray.

Words to use: String, dip, design, pattern; names of colors.

1. Let the child dip the string into the paint, holding onto one end, then drag the wet string across the paper to form designs.

2. Encourage the child to use several pieces of string dipped in different colors to vary the design.

3. Try using different types of string, thread, and yarn to make different widths of line and different textures.

4. Use string painting in combination with spatter and/or sponge painting for interesting results.

(87) FOLDING PAPER

Materials: Paper, scissors, paste.

Words to use: Rectangle, triangle, fold.

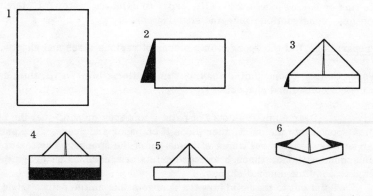

1. Hat: Use a rectangular (not square) piece of paper. Fold it in half. Fold the left and right corners in towards the center to make a

triangle on top. Fold the bottom strip up on each side to leave an opening at the bottom.

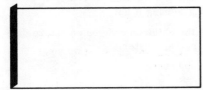

2. Fan: Cut a piece of paper so that it is much longer from left to right than from top to bottom. Fold one end over about $\frac{1}{2}$ in. Fold it back the other way the same amount. Continue until the entire paper is folded. Hold the bottom tight and fan out the top. To keep the bottom together, paste a small strip of paper around it.

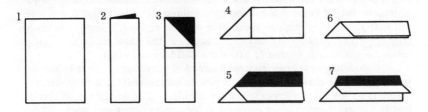

3. Airplane: Use a rectangular (not square) piece of paper. Fold it in half the long way. Fold one corner towards the center as shown. Do the same on the opposite side to form a point. Fold the sides down so that the edges meet at the center fold, making wings that stick out. A paper clip can be attached to the nose for better flying.

88 COLLAGE

Materials: Cardboard for background—shirt cardboards, tops of boxes, paper or plastic meat trays, and the like; glue; tempera paint (optional); peas, beans, macaroni (see Preparation), nutshells, cereal, bottle caps, string, cloth, cotton, paper, and other materials with interesting texture and form.

Preparation: To make colored macaroni for a collage, mix food coloring with warm water and place macaroni in it for a few minutes (don't let it get soggy). Take out the macaroni and spread it on a paper towel to dry.

Words to use: Collage, names of materials used.

1. Let the child choose from the materials you have set out for him. Show him how to glue the objects onto the cardboard. Paint can be added to the collage before, after, or during the gluing process. Let the collage dry thoroughly before attempting to hang it up.

2. Keep a "collage box" where the children and you can store discardable items that might be useful as collage material.

 PLAYDOUGH

Materials: Playdough (see Preparation), cookie cutters, spoon, dulledged knife, plastic dishes, toothpicks, paper cups, toy roller or pastry roller.

Preparation: Playdough can be bought, or made with the following recipe: Mix 3 cups flour, 1 cup salt, and $\frac{1}{2}$ cup water to doughlike consistency. A drop or two of vegetable oil and food coloring can be added if you like (oil may cause the dough to spoil after a week or two). Store it in the refrigerator in a plastic bag or can. Keep covered when not in use. (If you make the playdough yourself, allow the children to help.)

Modeling clay may be used instead of playdough, but it is not as easy for a little child to handle. If you do let the child use clay, first soften it up for him by kneading it for a while. The advantage of clay is that it will not harden when exposed to the air as playdough does.

There are also some self-hardening and oven-hardening clays available on the market. These should be kept damp in a plastic bag. After an object is made, it will harden in the air or with oven heat and can then be painted and varnished if you wish.

Words to use: Dough, mix, knead, shape.

1. Shapes and forms: Let the child roll out the dough with a toy or real pastry roller, then cut out different shapes with a dull knife.

2. Animals: Suggest different animals the child might make, such as a snake or cat. Let him use his imagination.

3. Make-believe food: Suggest that the child roll the dough into little balls for peas or apples, flatten it for a slice of bread, push a ball in with his thumb to make a bowl, and so on. He can make a whole serving of food and then pretend to eat it or serve it to others. Make sure he understands that it is just make-believe food and must not be eaten.

4. Jewelry: Have the child form rings, bracelets, and necklaces.

Note: If the objects made out of playdough are left exposed to the air, they will harden.

(90) MAKING PRINTS

Materials: Potato, paint or ink, brush, paper; construction paper and shelving paper.

Preparation: Cut the potato in half. Make a simple design by cutting away 1/8-1/4 in. around the outside of the shape. You can also use other vegetables and fruit for making printing blocks, for instance, carrots and turnips.

Words to use: Print, design, light, dark.

1. Let the child dip the brush into ink or paint, rub the brush over the potato design, and press it on paper. The more times he presses before rebrushing, the lighter the design will be. Encourage the child to use other colors and designs.

2. The child can use the printing technique to design greeting cards on construction paper and make gift-wrapping paper from shelving paper.

(91) BUILDING

Materials: Soft wood, hammer, nails, saw, screwdriver, screws, vise.

Preparation: Use a workbench, old table, protected floor, or some other appropriate work area.

Words to use: Names of tools.

Using a good-quality hammer, show the child how to drive nails into a soft piece of wood. At first, have him hit the nail lightly, until he becomes sure of his aim. Then let the child nail several pieces of wood together. He may have an idea in mind, like a truck or house, or he may want to make an interesting abstract design. Let him decide what to make.

Later you can show him how to use a screwdriver and a saw. Make sure the wood is held firmly in a vise and that the child puts both hands on the saw handle to insure safety.

Always supervise the use of tools. If you do not know how to handle them properly yourself, find someone who does to teach the child their proper use.

92 EGGSHELL PICTURES

Materials: Eggshells, food coloring, piece of cardboard, glue, vinegar.

Preparation: Mix food coloring with water and a drop or two of vinegar. Dye the shells different colors.

Words to use: Shells, glue; names of colors.

1. Help the child with the following steps: break the eggshells into little pieces; draw a picture on the cardboard; brush one area of the picture at a time with glue; then, while it is still wet, cover it with broken shells; shake off the excess shells; then glue another area and cover it with shells of another color, continuing this process until the whole picture is covered.

2. This project can also be done without drawing a picture first. Let the child begin directly by gluing the shells on one area at a time.

93 PAPER WEAVING

Materials: Construction or other heavy paper, scissors, ruler, pencil.

Preparation: On a large piece of paper, draw lines 1 in. apart beginning 1 in. from each edge, as shown in the illustration. Cut the paper on these lines. Cut another piece of paper of a different color into 1 in. strips.

Words to use: Weaving; over, under.

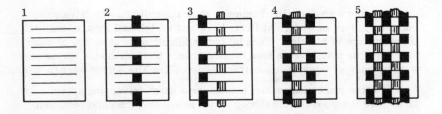

Show the child how to weave a strip of paper over and under the cut paper. When he finishes weaving, have him push the strip all the way over to one end of the paper. If he started the first strip over, he begins the next strip under, as shown. Let him continue until the strips are too close to the edge to continue. Show him how to spread the weaving out to fill in the space.

With contrasting colors, this weaving project makes a decorative placemat for the table.

(94) PAPIER-MÂCHÉ

Materials: Newspaper, thin paste (or flour and water mixture), vaseline or oil, paint, shellac; clay and cardboard (for mask only).

Preparation: This activity is messy. Protect tables and the floor with newspaper.

Words to use: Papier-mâché, rip, tear, strips.

1. Encourage the child to choose an object in the room to make out of papier-mâché; for example, a small bowl, a ball, or a piece of fruit. Let him cover the object with vaseline or oil. Assist him as needed with the following: rip the newspaper into thin strips; dip the strips of newspaper into the paste and place them over the object; cover the object with several criss-crossed layers until it has a good solid covering; let the project dry completely.

If the child is making a round object, the papier-mâché has to be cut in half to remove the object. If his project is a bowl, you can probably loosen it with a knife. If you have cut the project in half, have the child paste the two halves together with additional strips of papier-mâché. Then he can paint and/or shellac it.

2. The child can make a mask this way by first shaping it out of clay on a piece of cardboard, then covering the clay and cardboard with vaseline or oil and finishing with papier-mâché, paint, and shellac as above.

Note: Exercise caution when using shellac or other finishes. Be sure the room is well ventilated.

(95) SAND PICTURES

Materials: Sand or small pebbles, glue, heavy paper or cardboard; construction paper, scissors, and tempera paints.

Words to use: Sand, pebbles, sprinkle, design, pattern, texture.

1. The child brushes or trickles glue on heavy paper or cardboard, sprinkles the sand or pebbles on the glued area, and then shakes off the excess sand.

2. For interesting effects, the child can use colored construction paper cutouts underneath the sand and drip different-colored paints on the sand picture after it is dry. Make sure he applies glue both beneath and on top of the construction paper cutouts.

(96) PAPER-BAG MASKS

<u>Materials:</u> Paper bag, large enough to fit over the child's head; scissors; construction paper; paste; crayons or paint; scraps of wool, cotton, and other materials.

<u>Words to use:</u> Mask, eyes, nose, ears, mouth, hair, beard.

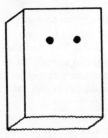

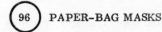

Fringe — Scrape with
edge of scissors to curl.

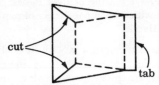

cut

tab

Ear—Cut on solid lines.
Fold on dotted lines.
Paste tab to side of bag.

Place the paper bag over the child's head and mark the proper places for his eyes. Remove the bag and cut out two holes for the eyes, then check to see if the child can see out of them when the mask is on.

Let the child paint or color eyes, nose, eyebrows, ears, hair, and mouth. Wool, fringed paper, or other material can be glued on for hair, beard, and moustache. Ears can be cut out of paper, folded, and glued on.

97 BOX SCULPTURE

Materials: Boxes and containers of all sizes and shapes; glue; scissors; tempera paint or magic markers; scraps of wallpaper, tissue paper, and other decorative paper; shellac (optional).

Words to use: Box, sculpture; big, small.

The child glues boxes together to form a sculpture of his choice, then cuts wallpaper and tissue paper into shapes and glues them on the outside of the sculpture. He can also add additional decoration with paint or magic markers and shellac the surface afterwards.

98 STABILE

Materials: Lump of clay or playdough; weeds, dry flowers, sticks, toothpicks, pipe cleaners, wire, pencils, rocks, marbles, feathers, or other items; tempera paint and brushes (optional).

The child forms a ball out of the clay, then flattens it on one side so it will sit solidly on the table.

Lay the objects you have assembled such as dry flowers and stones on the child's working table and let him stick them into the clay to form an interesting arrangement. He may want to paint some of the items first.

99 SHAPE JEWELRY

Materials: Scissors, needle, thread, construction paper, paste.

Preparation: Out of variously colored construction paper cut a number of copies of squares, rectangles, triangles, circles, crescents, diamonds, and other shapes. Cut the shapes about 3/4-1 in. across.

Words to use: String, necklace, bracelet, ring, knot; square, rectangle, triangle, circle.

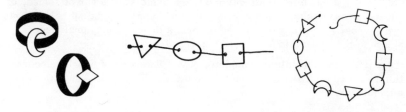

1. Ring: Cut a strip of paper 1/4-1/2 in. wide. Measure the length by wrapping it around the child's finger. Help the child cut it long enough to overlap and paste it together to form a band. He can then paste a shape on top for an ornament.

2. Necklace or bracelet: The child strings shapes on a knotted thread as shown in the illustration. Help him join the ends of the string with a knot.

(100) SHAPE MOBILE

Materials: Construction paper, cardboard or paper plate, stapler or paste, string, scissors, thumbtack.

Preparation: Cut a large circle out of cardboard or use a paper plate for the top of the mobile. Attach a long piece of string to the center of the circle, either by threading it through a hole or by attaching it with a stapler or paste. On the other side of the circle, attach five or six pieces of string of various lengths. Out of variously colored construction paper cut a number of copies of squares, triangles, rectangles, circles, and other shapes.

Words to use: Mobile, balance; names of shapes.

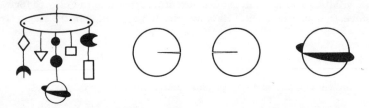

Hold the mobile by the long string and say, "Let's paste shapes on these strings to make a pretty decoration to hang from the ceiling." Let the child pick out shapes and paste them on the strings. Help him balance the mobile.

For a more interesting mobile, the basic shapes can be folded, or cut into crescents and other forms. By making a straight cut halfway into two shapes, they can be combined to form a three-dimensional shape as shown in the illustration.

When the mobile is complete, say, "This kind of hanging decoration is called a MOBILE." Hang it from the ceiling or in a doorway with a thumbtack.

(101) SHAPE FIGURES

Materials: Construction paper, scissors, paste, white paper.

Preparation: Out of variously colored construction paper cut a number of copies of four basic shapes: squares, rectangles, triangles, and circles. Cut them in various sizes.

Words to use: Shape, names of shapes.

Say, "Let's make a boy (girl, dog, house) out of these shapes. Can you find a shape for his head?" When the child picks out a shape, let him paste it on the white paper. Say, "What shape would you like to use for his body?" Let the child continue picking out and pasting shapes for legs, feet, arms, and hands.

Entire scenes may be created with animals, people, trees, and houses. Do not be concerned if the objects don't look like faithful representations. Let the child please himself with his creations.

(102) BUILDING A CITY

Materials: Very large piece of heavy cardboard, masonite, or wood; boxes; glue; construction paper; scissors; styrofoam or papier-mâché balls; sticks, dowels, or pipe cleaners; playdough or clay; magic markers, crayons, or tempera paint.

Words to use: City, street, sidewalk, building.

On a large piece of cardboard, masonite, or wood, draw lines dividing city blocks, streets, and sidewalks. Let the child glue boxes to the board for buildings. He may wish to mark in windows or paint the boxes first.

Help the child cut construction paper into strips for sidewalks and streets and glue them on the board.

Let the child stick dowels, pipe cleaners, or sticks into styrofoam or papier-mâché balls to make street lights and then glue them to the board.

The child may also want to make trees, bushes, people, animals, and other items out of clay or playdough and place them on the board. Ask the child what else he thinks belongs in his city. Let him use his imagination and the materials around him.

103 HAND PUPPETS

Materials: Small paper bag, crayons, sock, buttons, pushpins, styrofoam ball, cloth scraps, construction paper, scissors, needle and thread.

1. Paper bag: Use a small bag that will just fit over the child's hand. Let the child color or paste eyes, a nose, and a mouth on the bag.

2. Sock: Sew on or crayon the face. Use buttons for eyes or nose.

3. Styrofoam ball: Cut a hole in the bottom of the ball. The child covers his finger with a square piece of cloth and pokes that finger into the styrofoam ball. Help the child make a face on the styrofoam ball with pushpins, buttons, and other materials.

4. Paper finger puppets: Cut out small puppet heads from construction paper and cut two slits for inserting a finger. Help the child crayon in a face.

104 ODDS AND ENDS

A variety of interesting art projects can be made from discarded items. The following projects are a sampling of the possibilities.

104A EGG CARTON CATERPILLAR

Materials: Egg carton, yellow paint, brown or black magic marker or paint, glue, scissors, pipe cleaners or wire (optional), two buttons (optional).

Preparation: Take the top off an egg carton and cut the bottom in half down the center lengthwise.

Egg Carton Caterpillar

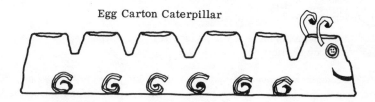

Let the child paint one of the half pieces of egg carton in yellow. He can then draw in eyes, mouth, legs, and antennae with black or brown magic marker or paint. Or help him prepare antennae and legs from pipe cleaners or wire and glue them onto the form. He might want to glue on buttons for more interesting eyes.

(104B) SPOOL SHADE PULLS

Materials: Empty spools, beads and/or buttons, wool or cord, tempera paint.

Help the child do the following: paint or decorate the spool; tie a knot on the end of the piece of wool or cord; string a bead and/or button on it, followed by the painted spool and another bead and/or button; make a knot after the last button or bead.

(104C) BUTTONS

Materials: Buttons, thread or string, large-eyed needle, heavy paper or cardboard, glue, crayons or magic markers.

Show the child how to string buttons with a needle and thread. He can make bracelets and necklaces this way. To make button figures, let him glue buttons to a heavy piece of paper or cardboard. The task may be easier if he draws a preliminary picture first, then glues the buttons onto it. Show him how to add outlines with a magic marker or crayon.

(104D) TOOTHPICKS

Materials: Toothpicks; styrofoam, clay, or playdough; glue; heavy paper.

The child can use toothpicks to hold small pieces of styrofoam or playdough together to make animals, people, and other interesting objects. He can also glue toothpicks to heavy paper to make toothpick figures.

104E POPSICLE STICKS

<u>Materials:</u> Clean popsicle sticks, glue, tin can, cardboard or heavy paper, paint or shellac.

To make a bud vase or pencil holder, help the child glue popsicle sticks to the outside of a tin can. He can then paint and/or shellac them for a final touch. Show the child how to glue popsicle sticks to cardboard or heavy paper to make shapes, people, dogs, houses, or other objects. He can paint them afterwards if he wishes. Let him also experiment with gluing the popsicle sticks to each other to form different shapes or objects.

Note: Exercise caution when using shellac or other finishes. Be sure the room is well ventilated.

Appendix

MATERIALS, EQUIPMENT, AND TEACHING AIDS

1. <u>Paste and glue:</u> Use small cream dispensers (such as are used in restaurants) or bottle- or jar-tops to hold paste. For glue, try filling a plastic ketchup bottle about halfway. Keep the hole open by squeezing the bottle lightly before putting it away.

2. <u>Food cans and boxes:</u> Be sure the edges are smooth. Food cans and boxes make good learning tools. The labels may be left on for color and picture recognition. Use them for size-comparison games. Have the children set up a make-believe grocery store with them. Empty boxes are also useful for building.

3. <u>Sponges:</u> Use sponges for sponge painting and building. They also make cleanup time easier and more fun.

4. <u>Clothesline:</u> An indoor clothesline is a good place to dry paintings. Clip clothespins will hold the pictures without damaging them. Spread newspapers underneath the line to prevent dripping on the floor.

5. <u>Storage shelves:</u> Provide the children with a place to store games and materials. Shelving can be made by placing boards across bricks or cement blocks. Be sure the shelves are stable and not too high.

6. <u>Shoe-box blocks:</u> Use boxes of different sizes. Cover them with adhesive-backed paper. For greater strength, insert interlocked cardboard pieces.

7. <u>Easel:</u> Attach a 3 ft. x 3 ft. piece of plywood to a tripod low enough for a child to reach easily. (If you do not have a tripod, attach the plywood to the wall at an angle. In order to make this angle, first glue on a 4 in. strip of wood to the bottom back of the plywood.) Nail or glue a strip of wood to the bottom front of the easel to make a tray for paint cups. Glue a thinner strip all the way around the tray to keep paint cups from sliding off. Use clothespins or large clips to hold paper on the easel. (See illustration on the next page.)

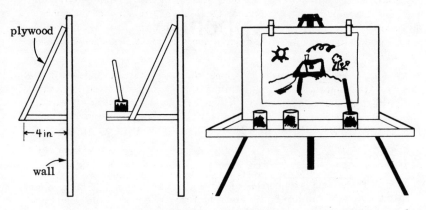

8. <u>Lacing and tying board:</u> Punch holes in a piece of heavy cardboard in two parallel rows. Lace an extra-long shoelace through the first two bottom holes and tape the lace on the back. The child can practice lacing it all the way up and tying it in a bow at the top.

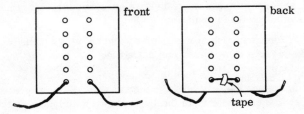

9. <u>Button, snap, and zipper board:</u> Use a large, heavy piece of cardboard. Take two small pieces of heavy cloth. Sew a button on the end of one and make a buttonhole in the other. Glue or staple the ends of the material to the board so that the overlap can be buttoned. Do the same with snaps and a zipper.

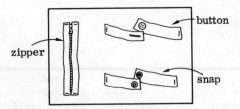

10. <u>Flannel board:</u> Cover a 2 ft. x 3 ft. board with flannel or felt. Cut out shapes from flannel or felt of other colors. They will cling to the board. The child can arrange them in interesting patterns. For

variation, let the child cut out his own shapes. Pictures can be cut from magazines, pasted on heavy paper or oaktag, and backed with flannel or felt to make them cling to the board. Use the pictures to illustrate a story. Use flannel letter and number cutouts to practice letter and number recognition.

11. Store, play house, or puppet theater: Cut out windows and a door in a large appliance carton. To make a stage curtain, attach a string across the top of the large window. Clip a piece of material to it with clothespins or cafe rod clips. Remember to remove all exposed staples from the carton first.

12. Doll house or store: Stack small cartons to make rooms or shelves. Paint them or cover them with wallpaper scraps. For a doll house, make furniture out of small food boxes and cans. For a store, leave the labels on food boxes and cans and line them up on the shelves.

13. Musical instruments: Use coffee cans or oatmeal boxes for drums.
Take off the top of a cigar box. Place several elastic bands of different widths around the box. Pluck them on the open side to make interesting sounds.
Fill plastic containers with different objects (dried beans, buttons, marbles). Shake them to make various sounds.
Cut dowels about 10 in. long to make rhythm sticks. Glue sandpaper to one or both for a different effect.
Add knobs to wooden blocks so that they can be hit together to make sounds. The child can decorate them with paint. Add sandpaper to the bottom to make rubbing blocks.
Attach bells to sticks for shaking. Or sew bells to a piece of elastic to make a bracelet.
Glasses filled with varying amounts of water will make pleasant sounds when lightly tapped with a spoon or stick. Supervise this activity carefully.

14. Paper plate clock: Draw or paste construction-paper numbers in the proper places on a paper plate. Let the child decorate the rim of the plate. Punch a hole in the center of the plate. Cut minute and hour hands out of cardboard and punch holes at the end of each. Place a paper fastener through the holes in the hands and the plate, bending the fastener securely in back of the plate. Now the hands will move and the child can use this clock to practice telling time.

15. Color chart: On a large piece of white paper, draw a large triangle. Paste 2 in. circles of yellow, red, and blue at each corner. On the lines between, paste circles of orange, green, and purple. In the center of the triangle paste the white and black circles. Print the name

of each color next to the corresponding circle. When the children learn new colors such as pink or gray, make smaller 1 in. circles of these colors and paste them inside the triangle. Hang the chart on the wall where the children can see it.

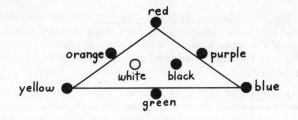

CHILD OBSERVATION CHART

	Child liked activity	Child finished activity	Too easy	Too hard	To be repeated	New words used during activity
Activity #						

Comments

Activity #						

Comments

Activity #						

Comments

Activity #						

Comments

Activity #						

Comments

Activity #						

Comments

Activity #						

Comments

References

BOOKS

Cherry, Clare. Creative Movements for the Developing Child. Rev. ed. Belmont, Calif.: Lear Siegler/Fearon, 1971.

Croft, Doreen J., and Robert D. Hess. An Activities Handbook for Teachers of Young Children. Boston: Houghton Mifflin, 1972.

Flemming, Bonnie, Darlene Softley Hamilton, and Joanne Deal Hicks, eds. Resources for Creative Preschool Teaching. Rev. ed. Kansas Association for the Education of Young Children, 1973.

Foster, Florence, ed. Adventures in Cooking. New Jersey: National Association for the Education of Young Children, Kenyon Chapter, 1971.

Grayson, Marion F. Let's Do Fingerplays. Washington, D. C.: Robert B. Luce, 1962.

Hymes, James L., Jr. Teaching the Child Under Six. Columbus, Ohio: Charles E. Merrill, 1968.

Landeck, Beatrice. Songs to Grow On. New York: Edward B. Marks Music Corp., 1950.

Lorton, Mary Baratta. Workjobs. Menlo Park, Calif.: Addison-Wesley, 1972.

Pitcher, Evelyn Goodenough, Miriam G. Lasher, Sylvia Feinburg, and Nancy C. Hammond. Helping Young Children Learn. Columbus, Ohio: Charles E. Merrill, 1966.

Read, Katherine H. The Nursery School. 3rd ed. Philadelphia: W. B. Saunders, 1961.

Taylor, Barbara. A Child Goes Forth. Provo, Utah: Brigham Young University Press, 1964.

Todd, Vivian Edmiston, and Helen Heffernan. The Years Before School. New York: Macmillan, 1964.

PERIODICALS

Day Care and Early Education. Behavioral Publications, 72 Fifth Ave.,
   New York, N. Y. 10011.

Early Years. Allen Raymond, Inc., P. O. Box 1223, Darien, Connecti-
   cut 06820.

OTHER PUBLICATIONS

Early Childhood publications are available from the following sources:

Association for Childhood Education International, 3615 Wisconsin Ave.,
   N. W., Washington, D. C. 20016.

Elementary-Kindergarten-Nursery Education, National Education Association, 1201 Sixteenth St., N. W., Washington, D. C. 20036.

National Association for the Education of Young Children, 1834 Connecti-
   cut Ave., N. W., Washington, D. C. 20009.

U. S. Department of Health, Education and Welfare, Office of Child Development. Superintendent of Documents, United States Government
   Printing Office, Washington, D. C. 20402.

Fearon Teacher-Aid Books...
The Idea Books That Free You to Teach

Selected additional titles in *early childhood education:*

COOL COOKING FOR KIDS: Recipes and Nutrition for Preschoolers; P. McClenahan and I. Jaqua. A comprehensive "idea" book on nutrition and cooking techniques for teachers of very small children. Management suggestions, recipes, resources on nutrition, health notes. 9" × 6"; 176 pages; line art. #1614–X

FREE AND INEXPENSIVE MATERIALS FOR PRESCHOOL AND EARLY CHILDHOOD, Second Edition; Robert Monahan. Over 400 items for early-childhood or primary-grade teacher to obtain free or at little cost. Films, books, pamphlets, posters. 5-1/2" × 8-1/2"; 126 pages. #3175–0

150 PLUS! GAMES AND ACTIVITIES FOR EARLY CHILDHOOD; Zane Spencer. For any teacher of preschool children; here are over 150 activities for readiness skills, motor skills, and more. All activities are easy to set up and manage. 6" × 9"; 160 pages; illus. #5068–2

CREATIVE ART FOR THE DEVELOPING CHILD: A Teacher's Handbook; Clare Cherry. A practical manual for conducting art activities that will enhance the young child's perceptual and emotional development. Generously illustrated with photos. 7" × 10"; 192 pages; illus. #1630–1

POTPOURRI OF PUPPETRY; Enid Bates and Ruth Lowes. An inspirational guide to puppetry in the elementary curriculum with a wide range of suggested materials. How-to illustrations and in-use photos. 6" × 9"; 64 pages; illus. #5500–5

CREATIVE PLAY FOR THE DEVELOPING CHILD: Early Lifehood Education Through Play; Clare Cherry. A comprehensive illumination of the value of play activities of children in a nursery school setting. Emphasizes physical and intellectual benefits of all forms of play. Delightful photos! 6" × 9"; 272 pages. #1632–8

COOKING IN THE CLASSROOM; Janet Bruno and Peggy Dakan. Thirty easy recipes for primary grades with questions promoting observation, knowledge of ingredients, measurement skills, safety practices, and lots more. Share the delightful diagrams with the children as the cooking progresses. 9" × 6"; 72 pages; illus. #1610–7

For a complete Teacher-Aid catalog, write **Fearon Pitman Publishers, Inc.,** 6 Davis Drive, Belmont, California 94002. Or telephone (415) 592-7810.